The Yoga of Relationships

Other Books by Yogi Amrit Desai

Kripalu Yoga: Meditation in Motion, Books I and II

Working Miracles of Love

Happiness is Now

*Amrit Yoga: Explore, Expand and Experience
the Spiritual Depth of Yoga*

A Yogic Perspective on the 12 Steps

Amrit Yoga and The Yoga Sutras

Love & Bliss

Books about Yogi Desai

Ancient Wisdom, Modern Master

The Yoga of Relationships

A Practical Guide for Loving Yourself and Others

YOGI AMRIT DESAI

Monkfish Book Publishing Company
Rhinebeck, New York

Paperback ISBN: 978-1-939681-43-0
eBook ISBN: 978-1-939681-45-4
Library of Congress Control Number: 2010936066

This book is a duplication of an edition originally published by Red Elixir.

Monkfish Book Publishing Company
22 East Market Street, Suite 304
Rhinebeck, NY 12572
www.monkfishpublishing.com

Dedicated to
Mataji

Urmila Amritlal Desai
July 29, 1937—July 31, 2006

In all her roles—wife, mother, sister and friend—Mataji was a model of grace in action. Tireless in her devotion to our lineage, she faced the challenges of life with a self-awareness few can emulate but all can learn from. Being in relationship with Mataji was a blessing to anyone who had the privilege to know her.

Contents

Foreword
by Lila Ivey, *Editor*

So often in his discourses, Yogi Desai begins at the end—with his first statement summarizing the topic of his discourse—only to circle back to the beginning, weaving threads of the middle and end, leaving students with a puzzle that is both paradoxical and abundantly clear at the same time. His teachings and writings are circuitous, simultaneously imbued with mystery and startling in their clarity. It is as if he is giving us all the answers we would ever need, yet leaving us pondering what the question was in the first place. It is for us to figure out for ourselves—the proverbial peeling away of the onion's layers. Once revealed, the insight he shares provides us with an enormous moment of "ah-ha!" In an instant, the resolution to longstanding issues is apparent. This preface will serve that same purpose—exposing the answer to life's most perplexing dilemma right at the top:

> *All relationships are based on the relationship we have with ourself, and ultimately, the Self.*

But how do we get there? Now that we have the end in sight, we must work backward to the beginning. Yogi Desai often says, "What you want in the end, you must have in the beginning." In Sanskrit, this is your *sankalpa*, your resolve, your deepest intention for integration. Alignment with intention is the path to integration.

Somehow we already know this, but putting it into practical use evades us at every turn. We know that everyone, regardless of culture, age or status, is searching for the same thing: love, peace and harmony. We long for that special someone, work that fulfills us, and children to adore. If the goal is so clear, why are we in conflict with everyone we care about and find ourselves shaking our heads at the mess we find ourselves in?

Successful relationships are not hard work, but they do require attention, acceptance and awareness. Attainment of this goal is indeed possible once we get out of our own way. The secret of successful relationships is revealed in the pages of this book. It is all about remembering what we already know. It is the remembering that is the tricky part, and putting that consciousness into play when we need it.

By necessity, this book is arranged in linear chapters. However, just as Patanjali's Ashtanga Yoga is designed to be practiced simultaneously rather than step-by-step, the secret to relationships is that all the following teachings are practiced together in a unity of consciousness when we are in alignment with what we think, what we say, what we do, and how we feel.

The inspiration for this book is derived from the first two limbs of Patanjali's Eight-limbed Yoga—the Yamas and Niyamas. Although they are listed in two categories, they too are not linear but simultaneous practices.

Yamas—Observances	**Niyamas—Disciplines**
Ahimsa—*non-violence*	Saucha—*purity*
Satya—*non-lying*	Santosha—*contentment*
Asteya—*non-stealing*	Tapas—*spiritual heat*
Brahmacharya—*moderation*	Swadhyaya—*self-study*
Aparigraha—*non-attachment*	Ishvara Pranidhana—
	surrender to the Divine

For the reader's reference, Yogi Desai's complete commentary on each abstention and guideline is detailed on page 99 in the appendix.

Observing the Yamas and Niyamas in our daily lives is a recipe for joy. Distilled by Yogi Desai's piercing insight and the depth of understanding he received from his guru, Swami Kripalvanandji, these gems of wisdom shine as brilliant guideposts on the yogic path of relationships.

Introduction

Fifty years have passed since I first began teaching asanas in the U.S. and progressively evolved my system into the deeper practices of authentic yoga—the return to the Source, which is our Soul-being. My early workshops on the significance of relationships took place among my small community of spiritual seekers at the Kripalu Ashram in Sumneytown, Pennsylvania. People were desperately searching for something elusive beyond the limits of the mind and the body, yet the more they struggled the more they remained mired in dysfunctional pairings, left-over resentments from childhood and, of course, distant unremembered incarnations that had indelibly marked them in this lifetime.

Since then so much has happened: an explosion in the popularity of yoga from a handful of followers in the 1960s who at first thought I was talking about yogurt, the healthful sensation from the mid-East (itself 6,000 years old) to the estimated 20 million practitioners in the U.S. alone in 2015.

Just as so much has changed, so much has stayed the same, as the saying goes. After a half century of teaching, I find myself returning to this topic of relationships again and again. When students come to me for counseling, their situations run the gamut, but at the core of every outpouring, I see that their distress is a relationship problem that has spiraled out of control, consuming their thoughts and their precious life energy. Literally an emotional death by a thousand cuts, relationship issues are at the heart of all human suffering—the misunderstanding of the roles we play with our parents, teachers, friends, enemies, and most of all, our lovers and children, those who are the closest to our hearts and cause us the most pain.

But who is causing the pain? Unfaithful spouses or ungrateful children? Neither. We are causing your own pain and until we acknowledge that fact, we remain caught in the grip of relentless recrimination. When others behave in a way we don't like, we make them wrong and continually blame them until we make ourselves sick. Over and over again, we replay the story in our mind, rationalizing our position and making another the guilty party. Despite whatever self-belief we cling to, by holding on to the conviction that someone else aggrieved us, we will never be free and will never be able to create the loving relationships we so desperately desire. Even after an event is long over, we continue this self-destructive dialogue until there is no hope for resolution. Yet there is always the potential for transformation. We just have to be willing to take responsibility and let go. Then miracles begin to happen.

Just as the foundation for this book is indebted to Patanjali's first two limbs of Ashtanga Yoga, the Yamas and Niyamas, I also derive inspiration on relationship issues from the great Indian scripture, the epic "Bhagavad Gita," authored by Vyasa. Chapter II focuses on a key yogic principle—equanimity in all things. This truth is the bedrock of my own teaching. Often it is difficult to be objective in relationships because emotions are so dominant we cannot see past them. Remembering the wisdom of Krishna to Arguna when he was faced with the task of warring against his own family, we, too, must dispassionately observe ourselves, accepting our faults and weaknesses, as we have unjustly judged those same frailties in others.

It is my heartfelt desire that readers will realize that the timeless teachings represented here are the gifts of the sages, Patanjali and Vyasa, and those of my own lineage of masters, Lord Lakulish and Swami Kripalvanandji, whose practical wisdom is as true today as it was 5,000 years ago. Read, embody and absorb. These truths have the potential to come alive in your own life and bring you back home.

With love and blessings,
Yogi Amrit Desai

Chapter 1

The Urge to Merge

*L*ove is the elixir of life, the nectar that nurtures every level of our body and being. Our inborn, evolutionary urge to merge compels us to search for love and the promise of completion it brings. We seek love in its myriad forms and in every expression of life, craving the experience of ecstatic union, where the walls that separate us from others dissolve into oneness.

With our first breath in, we arrive in this life pure and without attachments, yet it is an existence devoid of consciousness. As infants, we live purely in the moment, delighting in our own toes and giggling at whoever shows us affection. In these early years, our demands are purely biological. When we are hungry, we cry and are fed. When we are wet, we get irritable and our clothes are changed. When we are tired, we get restless and are tucked into bed. At this stage, closeness to our mother is not personal affection, but an instinctual bonding for the fulfillment of basic needs and the preservation of life.

It does not take long for the innocence of childhood to wear off. In ages past, it was said that a child was with God for the first seven years. Today, with the influence of mass media messages, it is closer to two or three years. By this age, the individual personality is already developing. The demands are no longer purely biological; they come with conditions because the sense of "I" and "mine" are very strong natural inclinations in children. Any parent of a toddler knows how conniving they can be. Parental and societal responses to experimental behaviors have a lifelong effect both on the individual and everyone around them. This is the beginning of the self-image we show to the world. Our self-image, or ego, is conditioned over time by our parents, society and culture.

We think of the self-image as ourselves. At this age, we are too naive to realize the falsity of this impression. We have no ability to separate the truth from fiction. The ego has needs; it makes demands. And when needs are not met, it leads to frustration, anger and resentment. We believe we are looking for love, but it is not love we are seeking. It is our ego trying to fill its insatiable void. It is at this juncture that the word *love* gets its bad name. The ego's hunger for more and more can never be satisfied, leaving us feeling confused and miserable. If we never reach the realization that we are not only individuals, but simultaneously part of the whole, we develop self-centered behaviors. This is natural and happens to all of us in varying degrees.

In short, our self-image creates the world we live in. We exist in a fantasy world, not the real world. Distorted by our perceptions, our happiness morphs into sadness, loving becomes revenge, and satisfaction turns into expectations. With duality comes unconscious separation. This sense of the false self develops separateness from others as it acquires definitions, concepts, memories and expectations of how life should be. Our immature emotions become a roller coaster of ups and downs, continually counteracted by their polar opposites.

This is a difficult trap and sometimes it feels as if we will never escape the cycle of disappointments. We repeat the same mistakes. We get stuck in our own patterns of self-destruction. But life is a perpetual therapeutic irritation. It is a school for learning our lessons over and over again until we get it right. The merry-go-round of life always gives us another chance to grab the brass ring.

Grown-up Children

The expectations of the ego follow us into adulthood. Adults have the same "I" and "mine" as children, solidified over the years through acquired associations from a collection of personal events, experiences, prejudices and false perceptions.

The "I" is needed to sustain the body. There is nothing wrong with it, but it is vastly misunderstood and overrated in terms of reliability. The mind is an extension of the body. The body would be incapable of exploring its human potential without the facility of the mind. All experiences of pleasure and pain, comfort and discomfort, are registered in the mind. This is nature's device. The mind can be our worst enemy or our closest friend. It is our choice to use the body and the mind as tools to explore both our human and spiritual potential. As we listen to the messages of the body, we must discern what it is really telling us, all the while remembering that the mind has a mind of its own. It is not beneath the mind to lie to us. In fact, it lies more often that not. The body – if we listen closely – never lies.

From our early pre-programmed conditioning, we unknowingly create an inner split. The "I" that originally focused primarily on nurturance goes beyond that role and becomes deceptive. As we grow into adults, it uses the body and itself as objects of manipulation for pleasure-seeking and pain-avoidance. Pleasure nourishes; but pleasure-seeking malnourishes. Pleasure-seeking behavior leads to indulgence in attention-getting through work, entertainment, food and sex. Protecting ourselves from pain builds the walls of separation higher and higher, preventing us from seeing what we need to see as evolving spiritual beings.

There is no going back. Once we grow up, we can never return to childhood and get the same joy playing with old toys. Once the light of consciousness reveals that this world and all its promises are just toys of the ego, we can never go back.

Moving Beyond the Past

Often, we unwittingly revive painful past experiences, bringing them into the present. Until we are conscious about them, we continually invite suffering into our lives, placing blame on the one who hurt us, both in the past and in the present. Essentially we are allowing that person to hurt us again and again in the form of another. We are trapped in pain that happened years ago. It is as sharp as if it happened yesterday. A new relationship—someone who invariably reminds us of the person from the past—is likely to reopen old wounds. There is no advancement or awareness until we learn to consciously let go of the past with all its blame and shame.

During my seminars, I teach through interaction during question and answers at the end of my discourse. Although it is a one-on-one interchange, the lessons of one person are applicable for all. On this topic of childhood trauma, a young woman once explained to me that she thought she had it all figured out:

Woman: *I decided a long time ago that I would never be dependent on anyone. I have been diligent about not allowing another person to be in a position where they could have control over me. I did not know where this attitude came from. It was not until recently that I realized through an inner child experience that somehow my father had created that part of my personality.*

Yogi Desai: I would suggest that perhaps you alter your language. Instead of saying "My father created it," why not say, "It happened in reference to my father." That is closer to reality. Remember that nobody creates anything for you, independently of you, or in spite of you. Remember that.

Woman: *Okay, I see. Then to say it correctly, "I realized I'm the way I am because I was hurt by my father.*

Yogi Desai: It would really be more correct to say, "Because I myself created this pain in reference to the situation with my father." As an innocent child, you were part of the situation. Even if there was abuse then, you are an adult now and have the power to release that hold. Understand that you did not come to this life empty-handed. You came with the baggage of unfinished karma from your past. How you reacted to your father was a continuation of your past karma. Your father may have treated your sister or brother the same way you were, but all three of you came out of it differently. A family lives in the same house, but each child has a totally unique experience with the parents. Why? Because we all are working out our own karma.

Woman: *I was so open as a child, but he repeatedly mistreated me with cruel remarks, so I shut down. At some age, I determined that I was not going to let him hurt me ever again.*

Yogi Desai: It was not only as an innocent child that you felt hurt. You are still hurting. You believe people are still mistreating and criticizing you. So, do not think that you were hurt because you were innocent. You are now very grown-up and intelligent, and still, you are in pain. Think about it.

Woman: *In reaction to him, I eventually developed a shell around me. I decided I would not give anybody the power to hurt me like he did.*

Yogi Desai: How did you overcome that?

Woman: *I haven't yet.*

Yogi Desai: But you have the facility to recognize what is happening inside you and that the pain is just as real. Seeing that is progress. The key to moving beyond it is to let go of the blame. Blame is saying, "He did this to me." And every time you say that, the unspoken completion of that statement is, "I cannot do anything about it."

Until you remove the blame, you cannot empower yourself to go beyond it. Your father was incidental. He happened to be your father. Unfortunately, he was not enlightened. How many of us had enlightened parents? What can we do about that? Nothing, but there is something we can do for ourselves.

You are also a parent. You are not enlightened either. You are just an ordinary human being. So were your father and mother. But you have the facility to recognize that fact and change yourself.

I'm sure Jesus had some trouble with Joseph and Mary. Joseph advised his son, "Go out and be a carpenter." And Mary, being a good mother, would definitely have liked Jesus to marry a nice Jewish girl. But none of these good intentions occurred. Instead Jesus ran away, leaving behind disappointed parents, who lamented: Where did we go wrong? Just as parents lament today. And look what he created for himself. Nothing ever happens according to what we want, but that does not mean it can be solved by blame. Despite his suffering and humiliation, Jesus never blamed anyone. His behavior led to ultimate freedom and victory.

Do not believe that it was only because your father was wrong that you made a decision to resist the world. You have not stopped making that decision. It just goes on.

Woman: *I can see that now.*

Yogi Desai: Until we wake up, we live in the same unconsciousness we lived in as children. We put so much blame on our parents, and yet we repeat the same thing our parents did to us. We do not want to take responsibility. If we blame our parents, then we do not have to do the work of healing ourselves. We have assigned it to them. Many psychology books firmly lay blame on parents. Everybody who wants to blame their parents buys those books and buys into that idea. It is a good investment unless you want to evolve.

Blame does not go away unless we are willing to take on the real work. Very few people are willing to do that. They will buy a book, but not take on the work of observing of how their minds are interpreting a situation, and how they are continuing to assign blame. The opening will happen if you first change your language, which will, by and by, change your perspective. Do you see how quickly the old ways of speaking come back? "My father hurt me. He did it, and I was hurt." You may have done that same thing to some of your loved ones, but you justify your actions by continuing to hold your father responsible.

Woman: *As a result of that incident and things that happened after that, I reinforced my basic concept. It carried on into adulthood: "There it is again. People are not dependable. I cannot depend on anybody. I am not going to open up." All that went on unconsciously. The pattern repeated itself.*

Yogi Desai: As soon as we become conscious enough to see how we replay a life event, we are also ready to drop it. You are conscious enough to recognize what you are doing, so how about being conscious enough to drop it?

Woman: *You cannot drop it until you know what to drop.*

Yogi Desai: It is simply the blame you must drop. No explanations or rationalizations are required to achieve this. What holds you back is not that your parents did something to you, but the way you took it and are still taking it. The reason we react to a certain event is because of our personal unfinished karma. Whatever our issues, we are back here in life to work them out.

When you have not finished a job before you fall asleep, what do you do when you wake up? You pick up where you left off. Death is a slightly longer sleep. When you wake up, you continue with what was unfinished. The only difference is that you forget what it was that was unfinished.

Drop the idea that your father was to blame for your pain. You interpreted it that way and there is nothing wrong with that. So do not now blame yourself. Just be clear. If you enter into self-rejection every time the problem comes up, then after a while you stop seeing clearly. Self-rejection shuts down self-discovery. You keep seeking the solution somewhere else.

Woman: *I will work on that.*

Yogi Desai: A mind that is colored by guilt, fear and blame cannot figure it out. A mind afflicted by charged emotions and analysis only justifies. Justification is not figuring it out. You do not have to solve your problem logically or psychologically. The most direct route is to trust in your Higher Consciousness. Every time such an issue comes up, make a conscious decision to let go of blame or guilt. When you do that, you do not continue to feed the problem, so it simply dies of starvation. All that is needed is for you to give it up. The simplest effort can be the hardest thing to do. But it is the only way—the *only* way.

Humans vs. Animals

Obsessed with experiencing all pleasure and no pain, humans set themselves apart from the animal kingdom but end up distancing themselves from the Divine. We have an animal body, a human mind and a divine potential. Animal consciousness is limited to physical survival. They live their whole lives with Fight or Flight reactions to bodily threats. They do not possess the free will to do otherwise.

Our identity is based first upon safety and survival, and is guarded with the same instinctive Fight or Flight response that happens with a real threat to our existence. We are perpetually on "high alert" with adrenaline flowing and brain chemicals pouring into every cell to sustain the self-image. This state becomes the state of mind we live in. Living in a perpetual high-stress situation ultimately damages our health, causing all manner of illnesses and disease. It is also responsible for flawed thinking and poor decision-making about relationships.

The human consciousness of "I" extends beyond the body into the realm of "who I am." The sense we develop as "who I am" is a vast, definable nebula of changing self-concepts, belief systems, personal perspectives, attitudes, opinions, biases, likes and dislikes, attractions and repulsions. The self-destructive ego-mind uses its negative influence to draw the body away from its natural protection. The function of our animal instincts is suppressed, sacrificed in the pursuit of pleasure and avoidance of pain. The self-image sets up an internal frame of reference, telling us who we are, how far we have traveled and where we are going. It decides what is right, what is wrong, what we fear, what we love, what we should ignore and what we should cling to. Whatever drive is dominant in our personality at any given time determines our perceptions, choices, logic, reason and even memory, which is distorted at best. It cannot be trusted, yet we blindly follow it every step of the way.

But we do have a choice to get out of the trap of our own delusions. Moving beyond the Fight or Flight response is what separates us from animals. As humans, we are invited to a third choice, but few of us take advantage of this unique privilege. The third choice is "witness consciousness." Often it is characterized as Wu Wei in Taoist philosophy. It is way of disassociating our personal reaction and observing an interaction from a third person perspective.

I, as an individual, have the choice as to what I eat and how much, and whether it is for pleasure or for nurturance. How often I have sex, overwork at the office, or expend effort to gain the acceptance of others are choices animals do not have.

All species of animals have group choices in terms of food, sex, self-preservation, means of survival and use of environmental resources. Birds build nests, even though each type has its own habits in nesting, in a tree or in a marsh. Lions in the wild live differently from cows on a farm. No two lions, however, will select a different kind of accommodation to show off, as if to say, "Look how special my den is. I am more prosperous than you." During mating season, males may battle to the death, but this is not ego. It is their genetic instinct for the procreation of their species, not because their ego will be stoked by being seen with the most attractive female in the pack. Animals have no individual ego-mind that needs to be better than the other. They are tied together as a group soul.

Each human, with its unique soul, acts as an individual, with the freedom to make its own choices. With this freedom comes the responsibility of the choices we make. If our choices only serve to reinforce the self-image, our karma ledger becomes filled with debits against our spiritual growth. As we grow, everything around us changes, but the memory remains fixed. Growing up doesn't necessarily mean emotional maturity. That depends on evolving conscious self-awareness. And that takes practice, as well as understanding of the difference between who we really are and who we think we are.

Identification with the Persona

Persona, the Greek word for mask, is the face of our self-image. It is not who we really are. It is who we believe we are. It is the face we show to the world. The mask changes with each role we play, whether it is daughter or son, sister or brother, mother or father, friend, citizen, businessperson or lover. On the stage of life, we change the mask with every relationship.

The exhausting job of continually changing masks keeps us in a stupor, preventing us from functioning at our maximum potential. Instead, we continue to rely on our underlying self-image, an adopted philosophical structure based on our beliefs, opinions, attachments and fears. We identify so closely with these concepts that we become them. They reinforce our gluttony for more luxury, success or money—none of which we really want to experience directly, but for the delight in how others perceive our accomplishments. The more we get, the more we need to keep us satisfied. It is a self-fulfilling prophecy. Identification becomes so enmeshed in our self-image that we will do nearly anything to maintain it. In its extreme, it leads to religious wars, assaults and white-collar crimes. At the very least, self-righteous behavior can spell our personal ruin.

We think we are alone as individuals, but there is actually a whole crowd of inner voices giving us directions...and all of them we call "me." For example, as "I" develops a complete identity, our entire experience of life originates from this fantasized self. If I am successful in convincing others of who I think I am, I also buy into what my self-image is selling. As I project this false identity, all my relationships are directed by a fictitious self. Ultimately, who can love a false person? This is why relationships fail, but without understanding of how we got ourselves into this predicament, we are left wondering what went wrong, who did what to whom, and who is at fault. Until we learn from these failures, we are doomed to strained relationships in our original family, extended family, love life and career.

Without awareness of the cause, we set ourselves up to repeat the same behavior in our next relationship, and the next and the next. We continue doing the same thing expecting different results. Does any of this sound familiar? Is this how you have been living your life?

> *You are the creator.*
> *What you believe, you create.*
> *What you create, you become.*

Chapter 2

Masquerade of Love

*W*hy do we fall in love? Because it is natural. It is inborn. As biological beings, sexual attraction is hardwired. Our animal body is pre-programmed to perpetuate the species. It is the ultimate law of attraction—the magnetic pull of negative and positive poles, yin and yang, animus and anima, Shiva and Shakti. We really have no choice on the biological level. As long as attraction remains at the purely sexual level, there is no problem. But as human beings, we have devised a complex system of mental constructions around what we call "love."

What we do have a choice about is romanticizing the attraction rather than allowing love to truly blossom on many levels. From our perspective of how we think love should be, we open a Pandora's Box of emotions, feelings and ideas about our potential partner. This is where we all get stuck, not realizing we are sabotaging what we want most.

Newness

New love brings new hope. Beyond the magnetism of sexual attraction, we are lured into the false promise of new hopes and new dreams. It contains the possibility of relieving the pain of the past and building a future full of projections and expectations.

There is a reason romance is called "falling in love" rather than "rising in love." Instead of elevating our consciousness, we essentially lose our balance and all sense of rational reasoning when we become enchanted with a new partner. This is the meaning of the saying "love is blind." We cannot see either the other or ourselves clearly when we are blinded by infatuation. Immediately, the mask of persona is called into play. At the beginning of a new relationship, the self-image is working overtime, trying to impress the new prospect at every turn.

In the early stages, both partners wear masks 24/7. We overlook habits in the other that would normally irritate us. Just as life itself is a perpetual therapeutic irritation, relationships provide the ideal environment for the therapeutic half of the equation to be instructive and not allow the irritation to become destructive. In the honeymoon phase, we pretend to like what the other likes, even if it is an activity we would never consider doing on our own. We refrain from comments that might offend; we go out of our way to make sure the other is pleased with what he or she sees in us to keep the attraction going.

Have you noticed how people in love are different overnight? Suddenly, we are most accommodating and easy-going. Nothing bothers us. We introduce changes in our lives we would never do under any other circumstances. Romantic love induces an extraordinary degree of temporary flexibility.

We possess untapped adaptability and willingness to let go of personal choices and habits like never before. Behind all this openness and receptivity is a buried desire to receive the rewards of such unbridled giving. This giving expects something in return. In its silent language, it whispers: "I will give you this, if you give me that." It is love with strings attached and a hidden agenda.

When we first fall in love, we unleash our imagination into the myriad of possibilities with the new partner. Hope and expectations are at the forefront of this exciting time. If we analyze what is really happening, we can see that the excitement is not so much about the other as it is about ourselves...and how the other makes us feel.

This euphoria is a natural high produced by the brain chemicals dopamine and oxytocin, and a host of hormones that create the ecstasy of new love. In this primal stage, the attraction penetrates no deeper than bodily sensations, even though our mind may tell us otherwise: "This is the one!" or "At last, I have found my soul mate. Now my life will work out." Dopamine makes us dopey.

The physical attraction becomes a psychological reflection. It is like the sun's mirror image in a body of water. The sun is not in the water, nor does its reflection change the chemical constitution of the water. They are separate and distinct, despite the apparent merging our minds perceive. It is the same with blind love. The surge of bodily sensations is so powerful it possesses the mind. The mind goes into a swoon. While this union is biologically induced, it is not consciously induced.

The Potent Power of Sexual Energy

Nothing impacts the mind as much as sexual desire. Because it is the nature of the mind to be doubtful, judging and suspicious, when it participates fully in the sex act, all inhibitions drop away. The total merging of the body-mind is experienced as a glimpse of cosmic union...and, in our hormone and emotion-filled haze, we call it "love." We mistakenly think we have found what we have been looking for.

This is why sex, more than any other desire, can so easily become excessive or even addictive. Sensual pleasures envelop us by totally absorbing the body, mind and ego. The merging of opposite energies in the throes of sexual orgasm temporarily remove us from the separation we suffer in all other expressions of life. Time stops; surroundings blur; thoughts cease; the mind disappears. The less the mind is involved, the more satisfying the experience. An explosive release of prana on multiple planes occurs simultaneously and spontaneously. This total absorption is the most engaging experience one can have. It is a glimpse of *samadhi*. The dissolving of the boundaries and subsequent merging of two individuals gives us the illusion of unity. But this all-encompassing experience is only at the physical level. Psychological and personality differences are not even broached. They are irrelevant in the explosion of ecstasy.

Sex is not love. It can be a step toward love, but it is only a small step. In this regard, sex is like sleep. Both are devices of Mother Nature. They absorb us in primal unity. They provide release and rejuvenation, but they are unconscious acts and merely restore us for the next day. No matter how much sex...or sleep... we get, we will never get enlightened this way.

Yet this glimpse of love's potential compels us to want more. We believe it is the beloved we long for, but it is really the experience of unity we desire. In truth, the lover does not bring the beloved to orgasm. The lover is merely the catalyst. We are each responsible for our own orgasm. It is the state of mind and body, a willingness to surrender completely to the rush of senses that produces the climax. This glimpse is enough to keep us in relationships for that reason alone, never exploring the role our mate may have in helping us explore our divine potential.

There is nothing wrong with sex itself. It is the way we use it that causes problems. Sexual energy in and of itself is not negative or destructive. In fact, sexual energy is divine energy that is being released downward and out, rather than drawn inward and up. This is the core of *Brahmacharya*, the conscious use of sexual energy. The intention in yogic practices is to manage energy consciously, not to suppress it. Suppression of sex altogether is neither necessary nor conscious. Rarely can it be achieved. There is no need to suppress sex. The aim of self-actualization is to channel every drop of energy at our disposal in a conscious and deliberate manner.

Yet passion is greedy. It is always hungry for more. This is when the mind, the self-image, gets involved and begins to sabotage the budding relationship. The mind starts planning and plotting for more. Efforts to achieve sex are actually obstructions. Again, it is like sleep. The more we struggle, the harder it is to fall asleep. The more we strategize an orgasm, the harder it is to achieve. The self-image must get out of the way. We don't have to do anything. In fact, total relaxation into the experience is a prerequisite to lovemaking. There is nothing to achieve.

As a relationship matures, the prominence of sexual desire is diminished. If it is the key element in a relationship, its fulfillment will also be diminished.

But achievement is the primary motivator of the self-image. Sooner or later, the self-image can no longer sit by and the mental constructions—the elements of destruction—begin to work themselves into the relationship, separating the lover and the beloved.

Dropping the Persona

The mask of the self-image may have many faces, but it is transparent. Acting out a role is physically and mentally exhausting, and within a certain amount of time, the newness erodes and reality sets in. Studies of the brain show that in most cases the "cocktail of hormones" instigating and sustaining romance start to wear off after about 18 months. When we are not compelled to behave according to nature's love chemicals, we have to start being ourselves.

As the newness starts to erode, the lover loses his charm. Or does he? Perhaps his faults are in the perceiver. Biological love energies drown the mind until the newness fades. Every experience must go through perpetual change—there is no way to stop it. So instead of experiencing love, we experience conflict. The object of experience changes, and the subject also changes. We think the other has changed, but we are still the same. But this is misguided thinking...both object and subject are continually in flux; sometimes toward each other, sometimes away from another. We remain attracted to the beginning of the relationship, but we're not so thrilled with the way things are going midway through.

The first thing a relationship does is show you everything about yourself that you do not want to see. It also shows you everything about the other person that you never expected to see. As the relationship grows, dreams gradually die.

At this juncture, there are two options: separate or stay together. Regardless of the choice, the equilibrium of the relationship has shifted. Sex is no longer the focal point and the partners will have to determine how much they wish to invest in making the relationship succeed.

When we enter a relationship, the other person is destined to straighten us out. No one ever needs to go into therapy or see a psychiatrist. We just need to fall in love. Most people enter a relationship to feel better than the way they are feeling right now. They don't want to be lonely. They want to get married and have children, as if this is the answer. They promise themselves: "If I can just find someone to love me, then I'll become whole."

When difficulties arise in such relationships, it is not love that causes the problems; it's what we were expecting love to do. Until we are conscious about developing a loving relationship, we all try to make love work exclusively for our needs.

So many people don't think about the course of their relationship until they feel miserable, unhappy or stressed. All they wanted was somebody to understand them and tell them they are wonderful. They want somebody to love them out of their misery. Yes, another person can do that, but only temporarily.

All that brings happiness or sadness
Will not linger.

Do not cling to happiness nor avoid sadness.
Leave the door open for whatever life presents.

Whatever comes,
Comes not to stay.

Chapter 3

Love as an Addiction

Addictions are not only related to drugs or alcohol. We can become just as addicted to relationships that give pleasure and relieve us temporarily from pain or fear. We manipulate people and external conditions to provide and assure perpetual pleasure, success and happiness.

When a loving relationship becomes an addiction, the lover becomes an object of dependency, the same way a drug takes hold of one's life. Dependency comes from low self-esteem. Inability to deal with life situations also results in dependency. Relationships can become a relief from stress, an easily attained gratification that is socially acceptable—and nobody will call it an addiction.

All addictions end up as dullness, unconsciousness and self-doubt. Beware: Anyone who deprives an addict of the sole source of their comfort becomes a victim of anger, jealousy or violence. The root of addictive behaviors is a lack of awareness of the all the Yamas, *Ahimsa, Satya, Astyeya, Brahmacharya,* and *Aparigraha.* In the darkness of ego-driven desires, we make up stories of deficiency about ourselves, which leads to desiring what we think others have and developing voracious appetites for sensual fulfillment.

Love is the complete opposite of addiction. Addiction demands that which love offers willingly, expecting nothing in return. Self-sacrificing love is the polar opposite of addictive love. Dependency makes both partners defensive and demanding toward each other. Apparent inconsistencies and dishonesty are often unintentional. All the attention and sacrifice offered to the beloved is only bait to catch the fish. Once the victim goes for the bait, the fish is hooked. The victims fail to see the hook inside the bait. The more tempting the bait of promises, the more hypnotic it becomes and the less obvious the hook.

When we are demanding instead of giving from the heart, offering only as an exchange, we have entered the marketplace of love. Seeing only our own needs and ignoring the other's, we become insecure. Seeing the other's needs, we become caring and compassionate. Born of fear, insecurity demands a great deal from the other. There is no way such demands can be fulfilled. Insecurity, like greed, never knows how much is enough or when to stop asking for more.

Dependency is like a vine that strangles the tree, sapping it of its life energy. Demanding chokes each other's growth, draining the relationship's vital force, leaving it lifeless. Craving more security, we find our own inner source running dry, and end up looking for a relationship as a resource to fill the needs. A relationship based on self-centered desire is bound to fail. The same relationship, when conceived as a commitment to mutual growth and fulfillment, is bound to succeed. A mature relationship is born out of the strength of self-sufficiency rather than from self-seeking demands. Love is the overflow of the self-fulfilled being.

Let go of what is holding you back.
Create space for what is coming.

The memory of the attachment formed during the illusory period of love is so overwhelmingly powerful that both struggle hard to return to the love they felt from each other. In the early stage of the relationship, when each one was focused on giving to the other, the conflict was planted as a seed of illusion—the illusion that what each one was getting from the other was love (rather than an evenly worked out exchange of expectations.)

Woman: *I understand how dependency and addiction destroy a relationship and the idea is not to become attached to people. But how do we actually achieve that, especially in the world that we are living in today?*

Yogi Desai: The world we live in today is not the world that is out there. We have no authority over the external world. It was the same 100 years ago and it will be the same 100 years from now. It's the world we create by our own fears and attachments. If we are free from demands, dependencies and addictions, we live in a totally different world. We are not talking about the world as it is, we are talking about the world we create and how to empower ourselves so that we create a world that doesn't involve self-caused suffering.

Woman: *It sounds so practical, but it's so hard to put into practice. How do we do that?*

Yogi Desai: We do that by not getting upset when we want something from another, but we don't get it. See if you can let go and let the other person be who they are. If you can let go of your demands, you have learned how to be with yourself the way it is, the way the world is. When you become aware, the whole world is exactly the same as it was before.

The only difference is that you have now created space for everything to be, everyone to be, every situation to be the way it is without you having a need to control it.

You are always working with the world that you live in. You create a different world of complete acceptance of what is, however your loved one may be. So many people are miserable because their children won't behave exactly the way they want them to.

What are we expecting? It never happens. For your parents you were "new age," for you your children are "new age," so what's the difference? It's all new. We have to learn to accommodate whatever happens without creating dependency. This is when you are in a position to cultivate a truly loving relationship.

Why? Because if you do not depend on any other, you automatically give them the space they need to live out their own experience.

If you are happy, it's not because you have what you want.
It's because you __are__ what you want.

Chapter 4

Expectation is Silent Reaction

herever we go, whatever we do, we do not meet life
as it is. Rather we experience our expectation of
how we think life should be. Expectations are silent
reactions. They are conditioned by our past and re-occur in the
present. Expectations are a way of seeking safety and comfort
to accommodate the self-image. They are our man-made ideals
of who we believe we should be and how life should play out
according to our perceptions.

As long as expectations depend upon the other person, love
is speculation, a hopeless hope and a self-projected dream. Expectations are extensions of our beliefs based on memories that
exist nowhere but in the mind: "I expected my husband to take
care of me…" "I expected my children to go to college, to be
healthy, to marry so-and-so….etc." and eventually the expectation of despair: "Why is God doing this to me?"

Relationships bring our expectations into sharp focus. Only
when we begin to see ourselves in a relationship are we really
able to see how our demands sabotage us. This doesn't mean the
relationship isn't working, but rather that it isn't going exactly
the way we thought it should.

Expectations are a set-up for disappointment. Hope is just another word for expectation. People feed on hope, but there is no sustenance there. It is as reliable as thin air. There is a saying, "I feel so much better now that I've given up hope!" What a relief not to rely on hope, which is merely another dream of the future. Hope is a false foundation.

Expectations of others are related to the attention and appreciation we want from them. What we fail to recognize is that others are forwarding the fulfillment of our expectations in the hope that we will, in return, fulfill their undeclared expectations. Behind the generosity in the early stages of romance is a file drawer filled with hidden demands.

Each person in the new relationship creates an illusion of kindness and giving to the other, but underneath is a needy insecure individual. This illusion gives a boost to our dreams for the future, but manufactures new expectations, further increasing the ecstasy of what each thinks we are receiving from the other. We expect this illusory charade to be free, with no cost attached, but this giving is an investment in which each is expecting to reclaim more than they are giving. It is not love, but a contractual arrangement.

Being in a relationship does not mean the end of all problems. How can we expect that problems will end as soon as we are settled in a relationship? This is all part of the dream the mind devises. The no-problem part usually lasts a few days or a few months. After that we aimlessly search for that harmony which can never be found by trying to change others. This never works. Your parents tried to change you and look what happened. Trying to change another is absolutely futile. Even if the other makes concessions and does it our way, what have we gained? A puppet who internally resents us. Soon we will tire of the puppet who responds when we pull the strings. Love with strings is a one-sided affair.

The Anatomy of Problems

Albert Einstein's famous quote: "Problems cannot be solved by the same level of thinking that created them" summarizes core yogic principles. For a scientist, he was a deeply spiritual man. To expand on his thought...any problem we have can never be solved by the same consciousness that created it. The mind devised the problem; the solution must come from another plane.

Any situation we face may have been initially caused by another, but we are responsible for prolonging it as a problem. Nurturing problems consumes large amounts of prana. Keeping a problem alive long after an event is over is exhausting; it takes a great deal of work to maintain a high level of emotional charge, depleting our life energy. Managing and conserving prana is essential in developing consciousness.

How do we continue to feed a problem, making it grow out of proportion? What makes a problem so compelling that we dwell upon it despite futile attempts to distract ourselves? When we find ourselves in conflict with another, who is responsible? Is it possible to have conflict with anyone without first having an attraction to them?

Emotionally charged conflicts may appear to be directed at the other, the offender, but we are really turning it against ourselves. We are the only ones who are truly suffering. We may have a problem with another, but ultimately, we are responsible for taking it to the level of crisis.

*T*here is an ancient teaching on the difference between pain and suffering. The analogy is that of being pierced by two arrows.

The first arrow causes physical pain. That is real.

It represents an insult or hurtful behavior by someone we care about.

The second arrow is our own self-caused suffering as we play and re-play the incident in our mind.

It is symbolized by the mind as it imagines what the insult or behavior means.

Making up stories perpetuates the suffering, which is not real pain.

Our beloved has probably forgotten the event altogether, while we wallow in our misery. Pain is acute; suffering is chronic.

Fear that fights a problem also feeds it through concentrated attention. It feeds not only our problem, it also adds new often unfounded worries through fear-induced projections and internal dialogues. When the mind creates vivid imagery of what is not there, it holds within it the power to actualize fear.

Removing the filters of perception, we can see what is really happening. Once we learn how not to extend the problem beyond its occurrence, it will die of malnutrition. What we don't feed with our attention naturally dies. Energy follows attention.

Communication between lovers that was once so easy becomes very strained once the masks are off. When the beloved makes a sharp remark or behaves in a way the lover does not like, he "sees" her differently, as if for the first time. Who is this woman? The remark may remind him of a hurtful comment from a previous girlfriend, a teacher or even his mother. The sting of her words resurrects a boiling pot of unresolved anger. He stews in his own juices. Her coming home late and not preparing dinner on time brings up the same buried emotions. His mind conjures up stories about where she has been and who she was with. He may lash out with cruel words and not even know why. He is caught up in reaction because she did not meet his unspoken expectations. Bewildered, she breaks into tears and runs into another room, slamming the door behind her. Her expectations are also disrupted. Who else in her past may have treated her this way? Both are left upset and confused. Now separated by hurtful behavior, the real story is not told. They seem to have suddenly become angry strangers. In truth, they are all-too-familiar phantoms from past relationships, either in this lifetime or another.

Expectation of the way another should act is self-sabotaging behavior. Reaction is a clue to one's own personality rather than defects in the other.

Reaction to what is outside is a projection of what is inside.

There are two types of reactions: the first is inborn instinctive reaction; the second is acquired reaction to situations we perceive to be threats. Instinctive fear and bodily discomfort protect us from threats to survival and ensure health and well-being.

Inborn mechanisms biologically program us to act before we think. Acquired fears bypass rational thinking.

Conflict in relationships invariably arises from personal reaction to what is happening in the present, but reminds us of the past. Acquired reactions are buried deep in the unconscious mind. Without rational thinking, we instantly evaluate and judge the present moment against memories or projections. Reactions are our entry into dualistic thinking. Duality is separation. The very thing we want to avoid, we unconsciously invite into our lives.

Any feeling of conflict is the result of habitual unconscious reaction and is not real. It is manufactured by our mental construction. The ego learns to adjust against reality by rationalization. These are devices of the ego that are caught when it confronts reality, and prevent us from becoming conscious.

All the accumulated ego defenses, along with rationalized compromises and denials, form the armor of the self-image. We live out of these restricted ways of expression that inhibit us from being totally present.

This limitation inhibits our full participation in intimate relationships, friendships and family closeness. Consequently, we feel deprived of intimacy and love. Hence, we look for love elsewhere by achieving more success, recognition and prestige.

Our search for satisfaction becomes more and more externalized, moving farther and farther from our inner source.

Duality vs. Polarity

Every thought, action and emotion is loaded with a tendency of repeated impact, particularly if it is injected with passion that is either "for it" or "against it." This is the very definition of duality. The difference between duality and polarity lies in manmade forces versus natural laws.

In duality, personal biases override the universal laws of positive and negative, expansion and contraction. The associated emotion is either "I like it" or "I don't like it." This is another form of the primal fight or flight response. We gravitate toward pleasure and avoid pain. This unconscious decision is where we create separation.

In polarity, we accept life's ups and downs, going with the flow of life. Accepting all life's occurrences with equanimity is one of the highest yogic teachings. Being content, *Santosha*, with what life presents, is the second Niyama. When we are in harmony with life events, we are also in union.

In the light of consciousness, we have a choice that is neither fight nor flight. The third choice is the important distinction between separation and union. This is "the gap." It is a moment in time that creates conflict or peace in our relationships. It is so subtle it is also called the "razor's edge." How many times a day do we balance on this fine line…once, twice? The answer is *all the time*. In every moment, we are making decisions, passing judgments on others, setting ourselves apart from what we don't like and clinging to what makes us feel better. All of these emotions come from reaction.

Reaction is not a deliberate choice; it is an intrusive compelling habit arising from the self-image. To be released from knee jerk reactions, one must learn the techniques that create space between what is actually happening and the formation of the reaction.

Unconscious patterns are first formed on the feeling level; then experienced on the thinking level, which then surface to the verbal level, and eventually to the action level. The more conscious we become, the more capable we are of catching the formation of a reaction at a subtler, primary level. Remember "the gap." Bring it to the forefront of awareness.

This is the point where we can make a conscious choice to grow from our experiences. Life perpetually moves us toward self-healing. Pain from the past is not present to continually hurt us; it longs to be consciously assimilated into the light. Every experience carries within it the solution to heal the cause of the pain of the past, giving us freedom and joy in the present.

Man: *I think I just figured out something with my situation with my wife...instead of rejecting these therapeutic irritations you speak of, I must embrace them in her.*

Yogi Desai: There is a subtle discernment you must first make:

Therapeutic is instructive;

Irritation is destructive.

You must not just embrace the irritation; you must also learn from the experience and change yourself. If not, the irritation has the power to destroy your mind with depression, jealousy and the perception of being deficient. Also, it is not about her, it is about YOU. You must be aware of the way you are reacting to her behavior. She is just being herself.

Man: *When that happens, I feel like I'm at my edge and I don't know which way to go.*

Yogi Desai: The edge is your first reaction. You have no choice about the reaction itself, but when you take action based on that, it is your second reaction. It is destined to create conflict. Don't go over the edge!

Man: *The edge feels like a space where I start running from my mind.*

Yogi Desai: Most of us run away when the situation feels too uncomfortable. Actually we are running into the door that is trying to open for us. We just keep slamming ourselves against it. Doors are always there inviting us to new possibilities.

Man: *If I choose a partner, who is in reality a reflection of myself, at what point do I stop viewing the relationship that is not working as an opportunity, but the time when divorce is the appropriate action? How do I ever know when I am reacting to "myself in the other" or that the partner is not right for me?*

Yogi Desai: When you dismantle and separate the reaction of conflict with your wife, what remains is just the other. When you see clearly, perhaps divorce is the best course for both of you. If it is still yourself you are resisting, you will divorce, marry again and the identical issues will arise. You are back with your first wife. You have to do the painful work of seeing yourself in all your expectations of the other.

Woman: *I am already divorced and I feel I have to save him. His religious beliefs hold that there is only one marriage and I have caused him this suffering. After years, I keep getting pulled back into trying to alleviate the pain I caused him.*

Yogi Desai: It is not you or the divorce that is causing his suffering. It is his belief system that is holding him and you back. Don't expect him to change. If you change, you will allow him to eventually change on his own, thus freeing you both from the bondage of a lost relationship. Accepting both the dark and light is polarity. Rejecting it, becoming either for or against it, creates duality.

Pain and pleasure are not truth.
They are the messengers of the truth.
Every judgment we have of the other
Is always in reference to what will make us feel safe
and comfortable.

33

Chapter 5

Loving without Holding

*V*ery early in life, I saw that what weighed me down and disturbed my peace of mind the most was holding someone else responsible for my happiness. When I would blame someone for an incident that made me unhappy, I became more agitated by that emotion than from the situation that caused it. Further it was a distraction from my highest purpose in yoga—realizing one's true Self. As soon as I recognized this fact, I decided never to hold onto blame or malice in my heart, no matter what others did. I never wanted to do anything that would disturb the contentment in my heart.

This abiding principle has deep relevance in personal relationships. But when we are in love or in a committed relationship, we forget that this truth applies to our beloved, as well as to those with whom we have only a passing relationship, such as in the workplace, traffic jams and the line at the market.

Relationships that work are based on our inner process more than on the dynamics between lovers. If we use the external relationship as a vehicle to transform our internal connection with ourselves, everything will transform. Only then is there the possibility for true intimacy and closeness with the other.

Deficiency Consciousness

When the other fails to fulfill our desires or meet our expectations, the natural tendency is to criticize or even reject them. Exclusive love invariably becomes possessive, which then resorts to control. The need for control comes from fear of loss. This unhealthy reaction causes both an internal and an external split. On the one hand we must be aggressive to get what we want and, on the other hand, defensive about protecting our freedom. When both partners play this game, distance develops between them that makes meaningful communication impossible.

The need for more and better (e.g., comfort, pleasure, security, love, money and recognition) ignores what is already present in abundance. Deficiency consciousness says: "I am not good enough" or "I don't have enough." These are lies we continually tell ourselves. It is not reality, but the work of fear, greed and attachment. It is the carrot we hang in front of our own noses.

Getting what we want and expect from our loved ones eventually reaches a level of improbability for fulfillment. What we want is symbolic of our need for attention, validation of their love, a device to determine their fidelity or, conversely, trust in us. Such subtle needs behind apparent demands are beyond the grasp of the one who is producing them. So how can the one who is supposed to fulfill them conceive of the other's underlying needs? It is a game in which there are no winners.

Even if our loved one was a psychologist, psychiatrist or social worker with scientific knowledge of the psyche of hidden motives, they would be baffled if they were on the receiving end of such demands.

Try this exercise to see if you receive what you want from another. If you consistently ask someone to love you, ask yourself, "Do I love myself consistently?" If you want someone to always trust you, examine whether you trust your own decisions all the time. If you want someone to always accept you, do you always accept yourself? What you cannot give to yourself is impossible for someone else to give to you. They cannot give what they want for themselves, let alone serve you.

A sense of deficiency builds barriers to protect what we believe is ours. Insecurity creates the desire to accumulate (*Aparigraha* – the fifth Yama) or possess the other, as if that will make us secure in their love. Yet the more we have, the more we have to protect, the more we must keep distance to defend ourselves.

We believe we must control or change everyone around us, hoping that one day we will have enough, and then we will be happy. The question is: how much is going to be enough? Does the need continue to grow exponentially and never end? When we get to the exasperating point where enough is enough, then we finally stop looking for more.

That realization comes either from frustration or from understanding. If it comes from frustration, we may say, "That's enough of that relationship," and start looking for a replacement because we think the "enough" had do with the other person. But when the "enough" comes from realizing that it is emanating from inside, then we can begin to change ourselves and our distorted perspective.

When you change yourself, the whole world changes.

Looking at the world through rose-colored glasses now takes on a whole new meaning. When you wear pink glasses, the whole world turns pink instantly. When you wear leather sandals, the whole earth is suddenly covered with leather. It all starts…and ends…with you.

We have all seen famous people who are very busy arranging their external images, and totally ignoring the price they pay in their physical and mental health to achieve all that status and celebrity. They think they're going to be happy when they have more money, more fame, more recognition or awards. All we have to do is watch the entertainment channels on TV to see the results. Once we have entered into such self-deception, no matter how hard we work, what we really want from life will be beyond our reach.

Prosperity is our Birthright

Abundance is as basic as our own body. Yet it is difficult to love the body. We ignore it as much as possible and just take care of the part that complains. It isn't until we have a headache that we remember we have a head. The only person who is grateful for having legs is the one whose legs were broken and couldn't walk for six months. Then he's so ecstatic and thankful. Somehow, we have to feel threatened or something has to be taken away before we wake up to reality. We are so unaware of all the gifts life has already given us.

The most subtle aspect of the body is the breath. If the breath stopped for a few minutes, we would die, yet we never pay attention to that which sustains us every second of the day, even while we are asleep.

Breathe, Relax and Let Go

The yogic term *pranayama* is composed of prana, meaning breath (or life force) and ayama, meaning to extend. Pranayama is mastery and management of prana. The intention is to retain more prana and prevent its misuse. It is a powerful means of clearing the channels in both the physical body and the subtle bodies, where karmic blockages are held.

Prana flows through the nerve currents of our body and carries out millions of intricate life-giving processes with precise order and intelligence. This wisdom of life force that works within our body unceasingly is at the core of all life-giving functions. Science calls it an "involuntary" system—yoga calls it an "intelligent" system.

For reference here, pranayama refers to breath techniques used to move into deeper and subtler layers of tension. It is also used to keep the mind steady as we encounter psychic, mental and emotional boundaries such as fear, resistance, criticism or doubt. When we breathe, relax and let go, our attention is disengaged from reaction. Breath now becomes a tool to remain fully present in the moment.

Through the practice of pranayama we discover the relationship between the breath, the body and the mind. We can see that stress in the body or fear in the mind instantly alters our breath. Consciously changing breathing patterns releases the conflicting unconscious forces that keep us from being relaxed and present.

The harmonious functioning of the body and prana depends upon the mind's cooperation because it is the processing station for all the inner needs of the body. The condition of the mind strongly impacts the condition of the body and the functioning of the five senses, as well as the prana that fuels it. If the mind is confused, prana is confused. When the mind is restless, prana is restless.

Where attention goes, energy flows.

Prana mimics the mind and assumes the patterns that are created in the mind and emotions. The movement of prana directly corresponds to the mental and emotional conditions that impact and control them. The moment we operate from unconscious emotional reactions or self-destructive thoughts, prana begins to carry out whatever thoughts or emotions we are assuming. Consequently if the mind is disturbed, it will automatically disturb prana in the body.

Unconsciously used prana is self-destructive. It creates psychological and emotional stress, which is our inability to recognize prana's relationship to our body, mind, heart and soul. The knowledge of prana's role in every expression and experience of life gives us deep insight into how to use all the levels of our being harmoniously, thus connecting with the infinite source of creativity available to us.

Slow Motion Prana

The Slow Motion Prana exercise was taught to me by my guru, Swami Shri Kripalvanandji. In the tradition of all great yogic teachings, this method stems from his direct personal experience. Realizing the nature of my work in the West, he taught me this ancient and secret technique, saying, "Teach this to your American students. This technique will be most successful and effective, winning the great admiration of its practitioner." With the blessings of so great a master, I have taught this technique to innumerable students for more than 50 years. The benefits they have received have been profound, transforming their lives on deep levels.

It is simple to practice, but profound in impact. As you practice it, the mind slows down and allows prana to take a leading role in directing the flow of body movement; the mind remains in a state of effortless attention. The body becomes the vehicle for the harmonious activity of prana and mind. The slow and meditative movement of the hands emerges from the inner command of prana; the mind simply allows the body to move accordingly. As a result, the body becomes relaxed and the mind effortlessly enters a deep state of meditation.

The Technique:

This exercise must be performed in extremely slow motion, accompanied by deep concentration on the flow of prana that accompanies the movement of your hands. The nature of the exercise is highly subtle, requiring deep attention to the inner movement of life energies.

Begin by sitting in a simple, cross-legged position. Keep your spine straight and hold your neck and back in alignment. Close your eyes and relax your body. Begin to take long deep *ujjayi* breaths by constricting the back of the throat, the glottis, to create the ocean sound. This simple breathing technique quickly brings inner harmony, relaxes the body and calms the mind.

After several minutes of breathing, focus your attention on the solar plexus, the storage battery of prana within the body. Imagine pranic energy glowing in the solar plexus in the form of luminous, liquid light. Gradually visualize this prana streaming upward from the solar plexus and flowing gently through your arms, wrists, palms and into your fingers. Your palms and fingers may begin to vibrate with the flow of prana.

Continue concentrating on the tingling energy flowing into your hands until you feel them being moved by the growing intensity of prana. Do not expect anything to happen. If your hands do not move, do not judge. Relax and allow the energy to build. Sometimes you may need to gently raise your arms to allow prana to move freely; let your intention guide your hands in almost imperceptible movement.

The key to this exercise is to concentrate on the prana and observe it working. Let your hands move toward your face in an extremely slow, nearly invisible movement. If you feel your hands are being moved without your conscious will, do not become alarmed. You are experiencing the flow of pranic energy.

As your hands approach your face, allow your fingers to move across your face, wiping away tension first in the forehead, then the eyebrows, press your fingertips lightly on the eyelids. Move to your jaws and nose and around your mouth. Gradually massage the area behind your ears and neck. Take as much time as you feel necessary to wipe out all tensions. As you touch each part of your face, feel the prana penetrating from your fingers, releasing deeply held tensions stored in your muscles.

Now allow your hands to return to their original position in the same slow almost imperceptible movement. When they have come to rest, remain in a sitting position with your eyes closed for as long as you wish, staying attuned to the energy flowing within you.

To enjoy what we already have is the most difficult thing to do. To be attracted to what we don't have is the easiest thing to do. The most difficult is digesting what we have achieved so we are happy and satisfied. To become disenchanted and ungrateful for what we already have is an easy trap. If we are not happy now in the present moment, no matter what we attain, we will never be satisfied. We will go on postponing happiness, looking for more and the right person to make it happen. This is the ego trying to conquer, control and manage everything in such a way that it is always in command.

When we have no need to control, defend or get more, then we can be happy. This is a very attractive quality and one that makes others want to be around us. It's like a magnet. People are drawn to those who are content and glow with well-being, and repelled by those who are discontent, downtrodden or depressed.

Addictive love is transactional.
Unconditional love is transformational.

Chapter 6

Self-Awareness

Self-improvement without self-awareness is self-torture. Awareness is double-ended. It comes at us from both directions. Like a boomerang, we send it out, only for it to return. Self-observation is a 360-degree operation.

We cannot be fully in a relationship with another until we know ourselves. To experience self-actualization, we must drop all identification, perceptions, expectations, prejudices and demands. We must be in touch with what we are actually experiencing in the present moment.

When we choose to let go of what we want without filters, then we can embrace life. Self-discovery is possible only through paying close attention and becoming deeply aware of what we are experiencing without distortions.

Self-sourcing never really begins until we make a paradigm shift from developing personal security of the "I am" to recognizing "who I Am." The journey starts when we realize we are not our concepts—the individual self-image.

The Grand Pronouncement from the ancient Vedas, "Thou art that" (or "I am that I am"), means that the Self in its original, pure, primordial state is one with the Cosmos, all there is. The

"I" that is changeless exists in a timeless dimension, alpha and omega. The "I Am" that has no dependence on external influence for fulfillment has true freedom and no need to control, manage or manipulate others to feel safe and secure.

I am not the thought I am thinking,
I am not the emotion I am feeling,
I am not the sensation in my body.
Because I am not my thoughts, my emotions or my body,
I am untouched, unaffected and independent from the drama I
call my life.

Self-awareness is:
• begun with the Mirror
• observed through the Witness
• integrated through Swadhyaya

The Mirror

In a loving relationship, everything we encounter in the other is a direct reflection of who we are. It shows us all we need to know, and what we resist most in ourselves. When we are in disharmony with the beloved, it is not so much the other we disapprove of, but unattractive traits we see in ourselves reflected in the other's behavior.

Just as we look outside ourselves for love, we also look outside to find out what is wrong with us. This is how counselors, astrologers and psychics make a living. We pay someone to straighten us out, when all along our lover is trying to do it for free. Everything we need to see is right in front of us. All we have to do is become involved in a close relationship, and all will be revealed.

Not wanting to see ourselves makes unclear relationships even more enticing in that we do not have to believe what is reflected, because we can blame the cloudy mirror. We attract what we deserve; what we are ready for at that point in our lives. This is why so many people have a filing cabinet filled with old relationships.

How often do we look in a mirror and symbolically throw something at it because we don't like what we see? This is what we do with our partner. Blaming others is throwing something at them for revealing us to ourselves. If we use the mirror correctly, love for the other becomes self-love. Acceptance of the other becomes self-acceptance. Unless we take responsibility, we will never change the source of our unhappiness. We only continue to make more problems in the name of solving them.

All issues of insecurity come up with the one person with whom we want to be the most intimate. The person we hold most dear is also the one from whom we want to run away. Love brings the closeness we crave, but it also reveals what we want to hide. It takes courage to reveal ourselves in front of another. These opportunities present us with both our most vulnerable and bravest moments. This is the paradox of love. This is *Satya* in action.

Love begins at home, so we must begin the process with the people with whom we are closest. If we can love just one person, no matter what they do, it will purify us all the way. Purifying ourselves on this level is the essence of *Saucha*, the first Niyama. Purification goes far beyond the superficial yet beneficial practices of fasting and austerities. Saucha slices through all the layers of the physical body and goes to the heart of love.

Anyone who has been able to love another without conditions becomes deeply compassionate. So much love emanates from them even angry people become peaceful in their presence.

The key that unlocks our own heart is locked in the heart of another.
Swami Kripalvanandji

If we can unlock just one person's heart, it is like unlocking the hearts of everyone around us. That one person's heart opens our own heart, simultaneously shedding light on every aspect of our lives.

The Witness

The Witness is that part of us that is non-judgmental and impersonal. It is also called non-participative choiceless awareness. It is dispassionate and disassociated with the self-image. It is not caught up in "our story." The Witness is our best friend. Just as the clouds move away to reveal the light of the sun, when the mask of the self-image is removed, the Self shines through. The Witness creates the possibility of letting go of identification with the self-image.

The key is to access the Witness as often as possible. In this state of heightened awareness, we become the Witness of who we think we are. Observe without the need to control anything. The desire to change according to personal preferences means there is still someone inside the persona choosing one thing over another. This keeps us trapped in past conditioning.

For the Witness, there is nothing to do, nothing to control, no one to manage. It simply observes everything that is in passing. The Witness enables us to understand the ego for what it is—a false identification. Observation must be practiced with compassionate detachment.

The Witness provides intuitive insights that help us see beyond superficial, superimposed perceptions of reality. This penetrating insight allows us to understand personal and interpersonal interactions and reveals the origins of problems that appear to be coming from others. Non-participative awareness is initiated by the penetrating power of insight and Witness. Self-observation is self-regulating. It does not cause the conflict that creates two out of one. Thus the Witness actually creates one out of two, or unity out of duality.

Witnessing opens the door to beingness. When we don't intervene by agreeing or disagreeing, then what we observe disappears into the object of observation. Being the Witness gives us permission to surrender, without pushing away what we no longer need. In the Witness, we welcome whatever presents itself and allow it to unfold without resistance. And in the observing, old patterns simply drop away and change happens of its own accord.

Swadhyaya—Self-study (the fourth Niyama)

This process requires turning our attention inward to clearly examine how habits, patterns and concepts have isolated us from others and separated us from ourselves. We must clearly see how our attractions and aversions rob us of the joy of intimate and loving relationships.

When the mind is quiet and free from addictions and fears, objectivity and clarity begin to develop. The invisible parts of ourselves will surface, initiating the deep-seated desire to solve external problems by probing the self within. The strength of our commitment to recovery depends on the quality, intensity and depth of our desire to make a shift.

The Self-discovery Process:

1. Look at yourself

Remember that you are not alone. There is not one "you," but a whole crowd of personalities that live within you. They deafen your ears with their conflicting views and voices. The crowd is made up of many facets of the self-image, each identifying with different memories of the past and expectations of the future, all vying for attention versus the Self that lives always in the present. Before you can immerse yourself in self-study, you must first ask yourself:

- *Which self is creating stress?*
- *Which self is seeking relief?*
- *Which self has devised a false way of escaping?*
- *Which self is creating isolation and loneliness?*
- *Which self is longing to be free?*

Vigilant reflection prepares the mind for the reception of real knowledge from within. Contemplation becomes meditation, as the mind is totally absorbed in the object of its pursuit. Soon all external aids, superficial techniques and self-help books are put aside and the seeker dives into his own being for all that is needed. Progressively, self-study moves from being an intellectual pursuit to meditation and culminates in a deeper knowledge that presents itself as a revelation.

Self-study is a leap into the unknown. You have trained for many years to live the life you are presently living, prepared by various teachers, family, society, professors and peers. Your new search for deeper meaning is just as immense an undertaking. It requires you to move your attention away from what you have spent so many years learning to a new relationship with what you don't know.

As you look into the Mirror of your partner and practice being in the Witness, you will notice that you have been more often uninspired than inspired. Inspiration that guides you toward spiritual growth happens only occasionally. It comes from the depth of your being. That is why it is called inspiration—because it emerges from an inner wellspring of spirit.

Natural inspiration is not for everyone—it comes only to the fortunate ones. Most people's lives are guided by their minds, so they are mired in the thinking process. Idealistic thinking is not inspiration; neither is inspirational reading, although both can give you the mental stimulus to do something worthwhile.

True inspiration is a rare and sacred event. Because inspiration is not something that stays with you all the time, what must you do in your daily life to prolong inspiration beyond its inception? Right action must follow inspiration. As you practice a healthy and balanced lifestyle through the Niyamas of *Saucha* and *Tapas*, you remove impurities in the body and mind. Then inspiration will naturally come forth more and more.

By not succumbing to passing moods and following your determination, you establish your consciousness, which carries through into all your daily situations. To stay above such up-and-down emotions, you must follow a discipline you can consistently practice. Then you receive the joy of overcoming your idleness, the *tamas*, laziness. When you break through that, and through the *rajas*, over-stimulus, you reach *sattva*, balance.

2. Consciousness Transcends all Aspects of Life

To become established in conscious awareness, practice it in all expressions and experiences of life, and exercise it through commitment and consistency.

When you make a commitment to your own Higher Self and say, "No matter what, I am going to follow my practices," nothing can stop you. You learn how to cope with self-deceptive thoughts and feelings that arise when old karma shows up and tries to steer you off course. View this an opportunity and be grateful.

As you become more conscious, you will be able to create not only inspired thoughts, but also inspired actions to support them. Combining inspiration with action, you realize permanent shifts in your consciousness. This will give you more initiative, trust and faith in yourself, which is the turning point for transformation.

3. The Pitfalls of Emotions

The area of your psyche where you are the most helpless is your <u>emotions</u>. They arise instantaneously from nowhere, blinding you. Without realizing it, you react without reason, and embellish the situation with imaginary details. Before long you have said or done something with literally no control over your speech or actions. Nor is <u>your mind</u> a good place to begin your observations because the 24,000 thoughts you randomly produce each day run away with themselves despite attempts to harness them. They connect with other thoughts and take you speeding away from where you want to be.

What you are looking for is a firm foundation, something over which you have some tactile connection. This brings you to your most concrete form—<u>the body</u>.

> *All energies needed for survival come through the body.*
> *All experiences of life come through the body.*
> *All emotions are felt in the body.*

How can you develop a relationship with the body to address all these events? The answer is through <u>attention to sensation</u>. In everyday living, you move through the day without giving a second thought to what is happening in the body. While much of the body's functioning is under automatic pilot, you remain unaware of its subtle messages. Unless you must physically exert yourself or become ill or injured, you forget about your body.

Renew your relationship with the body by bringing awareness and attention to physical sensation. Then the body becomes your laboratory, where you can conduct experiments in your own private space. As awareness develops you can then move this watchful awareness into your daily activities and your relationships. Soon you are testing its presence in all facets of life.

Physical tensions or reactions are the most detectable sensations you have, especially compared to the speculative imagination of the mind. Focus on sensation becomes a powerful tool to verify your self-observation process. Being consciously aware of the body's changing sensations is reminiscent of the old adage, "You never stand in the same river twice." Every experience is therefore new, offering another opportunity to see life differently. It is only past memories that persuade you to view life situations as the same. You have memories, but you are not those memories. When you connect with physical sensations through choiceless awareness, it reintroduces you to the self-healing transformative wisdom of the prana body. It removes body-mind conflict and renews the body-mind friendship, giving you access to the unified presence where opposites happen simultaneously.

Swadhyaya takes effort. It is a quest. Before long, fantasy and distractions of everyday living dissuade you from Swadhyaya. The mind re-exerts its authority. You may convince yourself that this effort is unnecessary or become disillusioned about the lie you have been living. Thus you discredit what you have been learning about yourself and snuggle back into your comfort zone—your circle of safety.

Swadhyaya also requires a tremendous amount of faith and trust to deny everything you know about yourself to be true, turn it upside down and start over. Your sankalpa, or intention, is directly proportionate to your awakened sense of *there is something more* to the life you have been leading.

When you get sidetracked, you forget to pay attention. You forget to observe. At first you readily remind yourself with enthusiasm. Then tedium sets in and soon you are re-proaching yourself for not remembering, only to find any excuse acceptable.

Be gentle with yourself; observe how everyday living provides distractions to your quest. With persistence, soon you will be aware of an internal shift, and yet be unaware of when it occurred. That is its magic.

4. Faith and Trust

The greater part of life remains hidden, unknown and un-familiar to the mind. To tap into this unknown experience you must rely on faith; you must turn to trust. This is a difficult transition because faith and trust are not functions of the mind. Faith is an aspect of the supernatural possibilities within you. The mind is human; but faith is superhuman.

Where the mind cannot reach; faith can.
What the mind cannot do; trust can.
What the mind cannot understand; faith and trust can.

Faith molds vision and nurtures your intention; it is the Higher Self working through you; it unveils new possibilities and new dimensions in life. The mind can become cultivated, but without faith you remain bound to the familiar and the known. Faith bypasses the mind to reveal the supreme possibilities of your own divinity. The groundwork of faith is self-trust and courage. If you do not trust yourself, you will not trust anyone. Self-trust is the basis of developing faith. Fearlessness is the foundation of faith.

When faith arises, one can live moment to moment without concern for the future. Life takes care of itself. This is the final Niyama, *Ishvara Pranidhana*, when you give up the results of your efforts to the Divine. With trust, you don't have to push life or make it happen. The divinity with which you were born is revealed to you through faith.

5. Signposts of Progress

With consistent practice, you begin to notice how much richer and deeper your perceptions are; communication is clearer and openness develops, you possess sensitivity you never dreamed possible.

Your attention will shift to pure observation, not on the object you observe. You will be attention itself, attention without an object. Pure attention is empty of all direction; it is free of memory. It is simply expanded awareness.

Observation without analysis or criticism produces sudden alertness. You will notice this first during a reaction, then before the reaction, and later at the moment of impulse. Then comes a time when you are free of the impulse altogether. Once energy is no longer projected as strategy, it returns to a state of equilibrium where everything remains peaceful and points toward that silent awareness within where all thoughts and perceptions come and go.

Clarity of mind brings about a relaxation from old patterns—a release of energy, which stimulates clear-sightedness. You live free from all striving to attain something or waiting for something to happen. If you do not comply with your old patterns, you naturally return to your true state. As the experience becomes more and more frequent, this stepping-stone falls away. When you remain the uninvolved Witness, there is no interference from thought or sensation; it is reintegrated into the silent onlooker. Object and observer disappear. What remains is your fundamental nature.

You have complete freedom to choose what you do.
You have no freedom to choose the results of what you do.
If you value the results for what they are,
*They become **prasad**.*

Chapter 7

Clear Communication

A breakdown in communication between two people is more about a lack of attunement than the words spoken. Words are often barriers. Language can be an obstacle to understanding. This is why silence may be preferable. It is love itself that truly communicates. Consciously attuning to another when there is conflict is one of life's greatest challenges. But without it, understanding is impossible.

Instead of trying to explain ourselves, it is better to open our heart to the other before speaking. This is the same as not reacting to our first reaction. Words cannot be retrieved. How often have we regretted harsh words spoken in an emotional state? The words seem to multiply and take on a life of their own. Who is then speaking? The insulted self-image or the real you? Take pause. Stay in the gap before responding. Attune to the energy of love if you feel too disconnected to the other at that moment.

Clear communication is a gift to ourselves and to others. By helping others understand, we provide openings for them to be who they are, which in turn, allows us to be who we are. There is no greater gift than the freedom to be.

Define the Objective

First examine the basic attitudes that underlie feelings. Coming to the understanding that happiness does not depend on getting others to behave the way we wish, but in transforming our internal world, changes every perspective we have on life.

People who suffer from the greatest miscommunication are those who see the world as the source of their problems. They think they are always right and the whole world is against them. They are always trying to change external conditions to solve their problems rather than working on themselves.

Accepting responsibility for our part in any misunderstanding is a quantum leap. If we are involved in conflict with another person, we should stop and ask ourselves: "Have I given enough consideration to this issue to ensure that I am fair and objective?" "Have I chosen appropriate language to communicate my feelings clearly?" "Am I coming from a place of clarity?"

If we learn only that much, we have created a unique capacity to express ourselves honestly and clearly. Whether others grasp the situation or not is ultimately beyond our control. We can only help them so far; the outcome may be uncertain. It is not about being right, but about doing and saying the right thing. Being in alignment with what we think, what we say, what we feel and what we do is the rarified air of integration. Communicating objectively with others without blame or shame is paramount.

Toxic Emotions

When we experience negative or unpleasant emotions, the most important thing to recognize is that it is normal to feel those emotions at times. We have every right to experience whatever we are feeling, but we do not have the right to impose it on others. Taking care in explaining a negative emotion can prevent a complete shut-down in communication.

If we admit to another that we are experiencing a negative emotion and don't want to project it onto them, they will accept it. They may even thank us for it, but if we explode in anger instead, we will receive anger in return.

All negative emotions such as anger, hatred and jealousy come from one source: we wanted something from that person and did not receive it. For whatever reason, they were unable or unwilling to provide us with what we needed. The more specifications we have about how life should be, the more occasions we have to become angry and dissatisfied.

Eliciting sympathy from others for what we see as problems in our life is a futile exercise. Sympathy may make us temporarily justified, but ultimately we will have to accept responsibility for our emotions. Accept negative feelings without spreading them to others. Rest assured they will not last. They are part of personal growth just as storms are part of the environment.

The next step is determining the origin of toxic emotions and what role our selfish interests play in them. If we are afraid to face negative emotions head on, we lose the capacity to be objective. Being afraid of fear increases its power over us. If we can face fear, instead of avoiding or ignoring it, it will never come back. Developing objectivity by being the Witness, toxic emotions dissolve on their own, for they are only the by-products of misunderstanding. They are powerless in the dispassionate eye of the Witness.

Try this exercise in creative communication. Follow these steps and see how differently the situation resolves itself:

1. Put yourself in the other's place.

2. Take a deep breath and open your heart.

3. Ask yourself: "Am I being sensitive to how he/she is feeling right now?"

4. Check again: "Is my heart open?"

5. Be aware of what you want or expect from the other. Always ask yourself: "What do I really want to achieve from this conversation and from this person?"

6. Meet the other person where they are at that time. If you speak at a lofty level they cannot reach, there is no hope of clear communication.

7. Speaking softly, gently and honestly, you will develop a silent strength in your language that has the ring of truth.

8. Watch your thoughts, taking care to harbor only kind, loving and truthful mental pictures. People who are in the habit of being manipulative or dishonest have very confused minds. They are always restless, tense and fearful, sending others subtle cues that they are not trustworthy.

9. Be accurate and specific when you speak. To generalize and exaggerate is very harmful to your consciousness because your subconscious mind is not discriminating; it takes everything you say literally.

10. Always speak and think positively about other people. This gives them freedom to change. If you criticize and condemn others, you are reinforcing their weakness. If you find it difficult to speak well of others, it is because you

don't really want to change. If you are willing to grow and to be flexible, you will allow that in others too.

11. Be economical in your speech. Say only what is necessary and avoid wasting energy in unnecessary emotional expressions. When you use your energy to express toxic emotions, it sets up a negative reverberation within you that others can sense.

If you can stay as attuned to the other person's feelings as you are to your own, you will be able to express what you are feeling in a sensitive way.

Timing is Everything

Even if we express what we feel with proper words, clear communication will not result if we choose the wrong moment and the wrong setting. The right moment is when we are objective and open to admitting our own responsibility in the conflict. Only then can we explain where the misunderstanding arose in a kind and loving manner.

If we say what we imagine will make another person accept us, we will only be speaking the language of fear. What we actually want will invariably affect both the words we choose and our body language.

Miscommunication is frequently a clash between two people trying to guard their security systems. If we understand what other people need for their safety and give it to them as a gesture of caring, we will have conquered many miscommunication problems.

Over time we learn to balance self-responsibility with patience and acceptance. As consciousness begins to awaken and we develop greater objectivity, we will be unable to place blame for miscommunication totally on others. We see that we have more responsibility than we thought for conflicts. Placing blame on ourselves is not the answer. Then it may seem we have more problems than before our consciousness began to awaken, but this is not so. We are simply more aware of what has been happening all along. This is an opening. As we see others through increased awareness, we also begin to see our own need for self-acceptance.

Developing Compassionate Objectivity

When we adopt an attitude of dispassionate objectivity in all situations, we develop the ability to see ourselves from the inside and the outside, without blame or guilt. Now we can see problems clearly. Compassionate objectivity is essential for moving from self-blame to self-acceptance.

Through compassion and objectivity toward others, we can also help them transcend their problems by offering new perspectives that only loving objectivity allows. Psychological techniques may be able to bring people out of their difficulties, but they cannot give perspective that will sustain them in that condition long enough to transcend the problem. Without clarity and comprehension, they will soon fall victims to the same problems.

With inner communication comes realization. What we perceive as problems created by others actually lie within us and, therefore, we are the only ones who can remove them.

Realization of this magnitude does not emerge at a purely mental level. It can only happen experientially, at the heart level. We may hear logical explanations over and over, but only when we listen with the heart do we know the deep implication of these truths. Then we see the change for ourselves that each new realization brings.

Woman: *When I get home, I'm going to try this new way of communication with my children first, because children are easier.*

Yogi Desai: Not really!

Woman: *Well, I would think so because a mother's love is so natural. It's easy for me to relate to them.*

Yogi Desai: Children actually have the most potential to push your buttons, simply because of the natural connection of mother love. They have an uncanny ability to get under your skin, where someone else's children would not have the same effect. In giving in to them and guiding them in the right way, you want to believe you are communicating, but this is not true communication. Doesn't it seem more like a struggle?

Woman: *Yes, I wish my daughter was here to learn this. I cannot get her to do her schoolwork. She resists me when I am just trying to help her.*

Yogi Desai: Everyone says that! They wish the other person were here to learn these lessons, but it all comes down to you and your ability to communicate clearly. It is your responsibility to help her understand without making demands. Explore why she resists instead of forcing her to study. Discuss her feelings. If you let go of your demands on her, you win. She thinks she wins, so both of you feel good about it. This approach creates the basis of your relationship with your daughter as she grows from a child into adulthood.

When love exists,
Communication of the highest order occurs spontaneously.
Flowing from heart to heart rather than from head to head,
Communication then becomes communion.

Chapter 8

Gratitude

When relationships run awry, it is difficult to be grateful. If we feel stress and distance, rather than comfort and closeness, the last thing that comes to mind is gratitude. This is the mind talking. When strife and suffering enter our lives from a strained relationship, how different might we perceive our experience if we embrace this gift life is giving us, and offering thanks for what we are receiving?

This is quite a change in perception. But in that change, a whole new dimension opens...the dimension of Grace. Instead of analyzing everything that went wrong or what we think is wrong with our beloved, we must welcome shifts in relationships as portals to this new dimension. Contemplate: What is life trying to teach us?

This is the essence of *Santosha*—the second Niyama. Contentment with everything as it is, no matter what we may think about it. It is living in a state of satisfaction all along the way. How often do we feel grateful for everything we have instead of complaining about what we don't have? What we have today, we didn't have 10 years ago or even 10 days ago.

Those who are content are not forever searching for what they think happiness looks like. They are not perfectionists; they are realists. Even when perfectionists achieve what they think they have been looking for, they are still not happy—they keep looking for more to fulfill them. Waiting for happiness in the future is impossible. At the end, they are still searching. The price of the effort is too high.

Realists know the secret to genuine happiness is being grateful and happy right now with whatever we have. It is effortless joy—joy without a cause. It comes from a deep wellspring of trust and faith.

Grasping for what we don't have is greed.
Gratitude for what we do have is Grace.

Receiving what we have from a place of non-ego is pure Grace. Do not ever claim it or take credit for it. When we are in this space, we not only feel full, others sense it as well. The peace that comes from grace emanates gratitude and equanimity.

Strengthening the Container

How do we contain what we receive? Think of Grace as a sieve filled with prana. If our container is weak, the sieve is full of holes, leaking prana as we complain, criticize and bemoan our situation. The stress of static in the mind is the drone of discontent, poking more and more holes in our container. These holes all have names: anger, upset, reaction, disapproval, resentment, and on and on.

Resources come from doing; gratitude comes from Grace. If we demand something from another, forget about it. If we ask with expectation, we may get it, but it comes with resentment. When we are joyful from Grace, all good things naturally come without asking.

Being grateful for however our relationship is showing up in any given moment guarantees that complaining suddenly drops away. Our view of life shifts. We no longer see issues in relationships as unsolvable problems. From a place of openness and gratitude, problems resolve themselves.

Living for dreams is in the future.
Gratitude for reality is in the present.

Chapter 9

Forgiveness

*F*orgiveness is an essential element in relationships with those closest to us and with the world at large. Sincere forgiveness is not releasing another for injury or insult. It is about healing ourselves—and acknowledgement of our role in the situation.

Ahimsa is most often defined as non-violence. But it is a much deeper concept than that. It is the active practice of understanding, kindness and forbearance in thought, word and deed. When we replace judgment with compassionate acceptance, ahimsa begins to flourish. This is forgiveness at its highest.

In the *Yoga Sutras*, Patanjali defines yoga as "the cessation of the modifications of thought." When thought ceases, the spirit stands in its true identity as observer of the world. Otherwise, the observer identifies with shifting thoughts. From this, we learn that the nature of yoga is a state of mental tranquility and spiritual freedom. Patanjali described five modes of shifting thought:

- *valid judgment*
- *error*
- *dreaming*
- *conceptualization*
- *memory*

Closeness with another engages intimacy, while it breeds contempt. A mountain range may appear beautiful in the distance, but try climbing those same mountains. The mountains look very different close up with all the rocks, crevasses and dangerous cliffs. It is the same with relationships.

When we struggle with issues regarding feelings of being wronged by others, we must remember that these thoughts are often unsubstantiated conceptualizations. They are a constructed image of reality, reflecting individual subjectivity. Let go of illusory concepts and focus on direct experience of the here-and-now, and the perception changes. Allow the mind to relax into witness consciousness, and the emotional tension between two lovers loses its charge.

Victim or Victorious?

Consciousness is achieved by entering the stillness of the Witness. In the center of tranquility, we move beyond identifying with shifting thoughts and material nature. In consciousness, we still live in the world and remain subject to physical consequences—old age, sickness, violence and death. Look at the example of Christ. He was forgiving even while nailed to the cross. He could unconditionally accept his suffering with fearlessness, strength and love because he knew that physical consequences are both an inevitable and incomplete reality. We, too, can choose to follow Christ's example and open our hearts to Divine Reality and embrace whatever is, as it is.

Because material existence cannot always be blissful, developing higher consciousness is the surest way to reduce pain and remain in equanimity in all situations. Resistance to suffering only increases the pain. Human suffering is amplified because we analyze it, assign blame and attempt to impose our will upon it. Pain recedes when we embrace reality, moving beyond likes and dislikes, while realizing there is nothing to forgive.

This is not to suggest passivity and lack of common sense. For example, when a woman (or anyone) is chronically abused, an external change is needed. Accepting violence and degradation is not the issue. If someone is inflicting physical or verbal abuse, do everything possible to create distance. This is necessary to see the situation with clarity and not live as a victim. Turn to the wisdom of Patanjali and his modes of thought: are we dealing with valid judgments, mental errors, concepts or memories?

These distinctions must be experienced in the present moment, in the here-and-now of events as they occur. When we realize that a situation is physically threatening, it is time for action. Create distance to establish a clear perspective and allow the other person to be who he is. This is not about forgiveness; this is a survival level issue. Doesn't it make sense to protect oneself? Isn't that ahimsa? When a tiger is stalking, run away; do not surrender to certain injury.

In most instances of conflict where forgiveness is beneficial, the mental tranquility and spiritual freedom of yoga is achieved by identifying with spirit rather than matter. To overcome false identifications, ask: "Who am I? Who or what is aware of my body, my thoughts? Why am I choosing to focus on these fears, opinions, desires and repulsions?" Remember, energy follows attention; energize swadhyaya, non-judgmental self-observation through witness consciousness.

Sometimes we must deal with mental errors, not only our own, but those of others. Rumor and exaggeration are commonplace; they are externalized mental processes individuals feed into one another. Patanjali identified error as false knowledge, a corrupting form of ignorance. When facts are exaggerated and rumor runs rampant, reality is abandoned and valid judgments are lost. No one can control the thinking of others.

Once we see that, we realize people's thoughts have little or nothing to do with us. Thoughts simply reflect the shifting internal states of the thinker, the mental or emotional constructs they choose to energize with their attention. When we let go of our tendency to assign blame or shame, then we feel completely free, regardless of who says what. Recognize that no one can hurt us unless we elect to take it personally.

When people are attracted to another in the beginning, they project their hopes and desires, empowering subjective expectations so they can feel safe. Later, they may express disappointment, criticism and blame.

Understand that in all significant relationships, we project our own unmet emotional needs and desires onto those we love. Think about how we relate to family members and close friends; there we will discover feelings, fears, longings, attachments and mental constructs. People's thoughts are constantly changing, coloring their perception, stimulating emotions and generating endless subjective responses. These reactionary mental patterns are not valid judgments; they are illusions, errors and pre-programmed concepts known as the veils of *maya*.

When individuals are caught up in these karmic patterns, their minds attack the same situation from many different angles. They are buffeted by conflicting emotions and opinions, frequently changing their mind. Why should we expect any-one to hold the same opinion about us today that they had years ago? We expect continuity because of our need to keep them fixed in their opinions. We fear the emotional conse-quences when others change their minds about us. But that is our problem, not theirs. When we forgive them, we give them an opening to be who they are. Because everyone is constantly changing, we cannot hold onto fixed beliefs.

I have a personal example. Once a follower of mine wrote a book filled with my teachings. Then for some reason, he became upset, left our commu-nity, and wrote an article critical of me. A few months later, he returned and was welcomed back with no reac-tion from me. I was very loving toward him; he started to weep. "I am sorry," he cried, and asked for my forgiveness. I responded, "What for?" I wasn't holding on to the past or negative feelings about what he had written months before. There was no need to defend myself or create any defensiveness in him.

I knew that whatever he wrote, positive or negative, re-flected his own internal condition at that time. When I let it go, I simultaneously created an opening for him to release it. When we don't forgive, we are holding onto our own opinion and demanding defensiveness from another. Relax, release, allow both of you to let go and move for-ward. This explains the power of forgiveness. Have enough heart to understand the dynamics of hurtful actions without allowing destructive emotions to take over. Don't think too hard about any of it. Remember, we are not our thoughts or what others think about us. When such disturbances arise, don't allow the mind to play with them. See them for what they are—passing clouds in an endless sky.

The process of forgiveness is simple, but not always easy. When a problem in a relationship occurs, it may be a blessing in disguise, but it cannot be seen at the time. The blessing is hidden in a treasure chest that must be pried open. The best way to heal is through the use of higher consciousness. For those who are unconscious or spiritually asleep, time helps healing. For those who live in memory, not even time is helpful because they remain fixated on the past. Why keep hanging on to something when it is over? Only when we let go of what happened in the past are we ready to do the real work of creating a better future.

History's Teachers

Sometimes these individual issues are found on a large scale, on a national scale, such as that between India and the British colonists in the middle of the last century. Mahatma Gandhi witnessed national exploitation and injustice in his country. He committed to oppose these abuses through non-violent action. He was not angry; he was an extraordinary example of action without personal involvement. In yoga, this is *vairagya*, non-attachment—love in action. Gandhi's actions pointed toward freedom, rather than being directed against the British. He resisted slavery through selfless, skillful non-violence, remaining detached from the fruits of his actions.

Criticism is not an effective response to injustice. Criticism means we are upset and impotent. If, on the other hand, we see a situation is unbalanced and believe we should take action to correct it, we are not being critical, blameful or angry. A true activist lives in a very different state of awareness.

Activists such as Gandhi and Martin Luther King, Jr. were dedicated to a purpose far greater than personal anger. They did not express judgments and criticism about injustice. They moved beyond ego and into higher consciousness. Here, they achieved clarity of purpose and intention. They understood that peace and justice can never be established by those who are personally agitated and blameful. Reactionaries are the ones who do the greatest mischief. Instead, Gandhi and King focused on ahimsa, and remained seated in Spirit.

We can follow their example by examining our own thoughts, fears and opinions, and by asking ourselves, "Why am I choosing to focus upon and energize these issues?" Then we can move beyond shifting thoughts and material nature. We can invite forgiveness and higher consciousness into our lives and apply these timeless principles to all, especially to those closest to us. As we achieve mental tranquility and spiritual freedom, we enter the bliss of yoga as union.

Woman: *I am feeling so upset with my ex-lover. Our relationship had really been over for a year before we finally called it quits. I was relieved when we broke it off and decided to remain friends. It felt right. But within a few months, he had found someone else. Now, instead of relief, I feel humiliated when I didn't at the time of our break-up. How could he do this? I cannot find a way to be in a loving friendship with him anymore.*

Yogi Desai: The mind will tell you all sorts of things about him and this new love interest. It may be true; it may not be true. But be assured that whatever your mind is telling you is not true.

Woman: *My mind keeps playing pictures of him with her. It feels like the life we had together is all a lie. It is driving me crazy.*

Yogi Desai: Your mind will certainly drive you crazy because it has a mind of its own. If you don't mind the mind, the mind is not a problem. Tell it to "shut up!"

Woman: *I know I let my mind run wild, but I am in so much pain over what feels like a secondary loss. I cannot forgive him for finding someone else so quickly to take my place.*

Yogi Desai: You don't know that. Did he tell you that?

Woman: *No, he didn't.*

Yogi Desai: So who is the one hurting here? Who is the one who is wronged? You are blaming yourself for not being the right one and him for not still wanting to be with you in the same way. You must give him the space to be who he is, regardless. Nothing can take away the time or the bond you have together. His relationship with someone else has nothing whatsoever to do with the relationship he had with you. Do you want to continue the friendship?

Woman: *Very much! He has been so much a part of my life I cannot see it without him in it in some way.*

Yogi Desai: Then just drop whatever your mind is saying about him and his new friend. Forgive him for finding someone else attractive and forgive yourself for feeling hurt and making up stories about the validity or meaning of your relationship. Let go of such thoughts. Do not give them any power over truth. Then you can move forward. The pain will go away and you can still love your friend. When you truly forgive with your heart, not your reasoning, you are accepting your role in the relationship and setting yourself free.

My beloved child, break your heart no longer.
Each time you judge yourself, you break your own heart.
You stop feeding on love, which is the wellspring of your vitality.

The time has come.
Your time to live,
To celebrate and see the goodness that you are.

You, my child, are divine.
You are pure.
You are sublimely free.
You are God in disguise and you are always perfectly safe.

Do not fight the dark,
Just turn on the light.
Let go and breathe into the goodness that you are.

Swami Kripalvanandji

Chapter 10

Conscious Relationships that Work

Our closest relationships reveal everything we need to know. Casual relationships that come and go rarely penetrate the core of our being. It is only in the arena of close relationships that personal growth is possible. For most of us these fall under three categories:

1. Marriage
2. Work
3. Food

Every day, interactions with these three relationships have the power to shape our lives. The juggling act goes on all day long with at least one ball suspended in air, while we hand off the other two, dropping them now and again. Awareness about these intimate aspects of daily life holds the potential to turn reformation of behavior into transformation of spirit, and treasured relationships into rewarding lifelong experiences.

Marriage

The major difference between getting married and having a lover is commitment. Any committed relationship creates problems because deep love purifies by its very nature. Just as the dross must be separated from the purity of gold, married love must be put to the test of fire. Used wisely, the *Tapas* of marriage can sustain you through difficult times, separating you from all your impurities as you become ever more intimate with your beloved.

The wedding is about dreams; matrimony is about reality. It is a sacred relationship committed to discovering the reality of life. All that life demands in every other expression is concentrated in marriage. The temporary aspects of sensual love give way to the permanent foundation of sustained relationship. The person we are will show up through the medium of intimacy. It will bring up all we have been hiding. In due time, we can no longer hide from ourselves or our spouse. The masks come off, newness wears away, the mirror is before us, so our attachments and expectations must drop.

In today's culture, we are more focused on finding the right partner rather than being the right partner. This is why divorce is so commonplace. If this one doesn't work out, we find another. In our unconsciousness, we are likely to marry the same person (in another body) over and over again because we are making the same demands over and over again. We must consciously choose to be the right partner by coming from a place of giving rather than demanding. The best chance of success in marriage is finding another person who has the same attitude toward the realities of married life.

Unconditional Love

In marriage, we must pay the karmic debt we have created in all other relationships. Every falsehood about which we have ever deceived ourselves will resurface. Our spouse represents the entire universe. Everything we have adopted that is not in alignment with the universal laws of oneness will unravel in the presence of the other.

We can expect nothing from marriage without first loving unconditionally. When we love the other without expecting anything in return, that is love. The cat-and-mouse game of "you give me what I want and then I'll give you what you want" ends. There are no winners in that game. Both win when loving without expectations or demands is the environment in which the marriage lives. Then, what we receive is enough, even as we keep on giving. When we love with an open heart, the heart of the other will open.

In life, this is a difficult practice between two people in a close relationship. What we want and need will continually arise. In dropping what we want, the possibility of clear communication re-opens. If we can give what the other requests, we are not giving away anything but opening our own heart. No one can steal what is given from the heart.

When we begin to share honestly, the distance lessens, and the walls begin to come down. This is the practice of *Satya*, the second Yama. Truth in words is superseded by truth of heart and pure intention. By and by, efforts toward openness bring us closer. Then we are not expecting love, nor do we require something from the other. We are simply giving. This kind of giving creates a psychological air where there is no threat, no fear and no defense from the other. If we approach someone without demands, their defenses naturally drop because they feel no unspoken threat. From a space of non-defensiveness, there is the possibility of unconditional sharing.

Giving is Receiving

Serving others is actually learning how to draw upon our inner resources. The person who can truly give themselves to others is the one who has found fulfillment within themselves.

Often we try to create more resources on an external level because we feel insecure inside. External security is symbolic of inner insecurity, particularly if there is attachment to it. When we serve unselfishly, all the resources at our disposal are used for others, instead of creating external security. Giving away our possessions is really ridding ourselves of insecurities, as demonstrated by the teaching of *Aparigraha.*

Just as it is the nature of the sun to shine, love is a self-luminous act. As long as we are not asking for anything in return, we close the distance between ourselves and the other. When we realize that giving to our spouse is really giving to ourselves, separateness disappears and unity emerges.

You are nothing less than the very extension of me.
I am both the giver and the receiver.

Love is the ultimate experience whether we are on the giving end or the receiving end. When love becomes a state of being rather than an act of doing, others cannot help but be drawn into the experience. Those who are in love with themselves shine with an inner glow that encompasses everyone around them.

Being open and receptive is a magnetic draw. Your partner will naturally sense receptivity. Those who are humble, free from ego and selfishness, become a receptacle—an empty vessel. Abundance from everywhere begins to flow into them in the form of grace.

Receptivity has a physical sensation that is associated with it. When you give, instead of demand, you stand straighter. Your neck lengthens, your chest expands. You exude a sense of dignity, strength, belief and acceptance. You feel you can live in this world free from any fears. This comes from giving away what you would otherwise like to hold onto because of habitual ways of protecting what you think you need to feel secure. In giving, all you really give up is fear and insecurity.

On the reverse side of receptivity is resistance. Have you noticed that when your partner does a favor with some repayment involved, you become suspicious and resistant? Your mind tells you, "People cannot be trusted." Their apparent generosity feels like deception.

Only in giving without asking for anything will another's heart open. Even if your partner doesn't respond at first, don't give up. They are working on their own doubts. They are secretly analyzing your motives, "What does she want from me?" Ask nothing, stay open and clear. After a few times, trust will develop and he will begin to open willingly. When you don't want something, everything that comes to you is a delight.

Never miss an opportunity to acknowledge your partner. Then they begin to see all the right things in you. Even when you say something wrong, they will correct the misinterpretation in their mind and listen differently, knowing and trusting in your selfless and receptive spirit. Even right things spoken to a defensive person will fall on deaf ears.

Marriage then becomes an opening on many different levels, levels that can never be comprehended by intellectual concepts, hearing with the physical ears, or seeing with the eyes. A deeper understanding and knowing between two souls takes place for which there are no mental constructs, words or sights.

Wedding Blessing

Love is a powerful force, a profound path and an evolutionary journey.
It travels through difficult terrain but rewards you with blissful vistas.

Love embraces both ups and down, the spiritual and mundane,
providing opportunities for it to grow.

When love awakens from dreams, it makes no demands. It gives unconditionally.
As enticing and attractive as dreams may appear, learn to anchor your love to the
earth. Give it feet to walk and wings to fly.
As long as love is unconditional, it matters not whether it walks or flies.
It fulfills both the practical and the spiritual.

It is the presence of love that makes one out of two. The undivided whole is the
nature of universal love.
All personal interests and self-centered attitudes disintegrate in its presence.

Unconditional love brings all conflict into union.
The moment you demand love, it disappears and conflict appears.
When you give love, conflict disappears and love reappears.

Love that unites is true love.
Love that separates is attachment.
Love is complete within itself.

In marriage, building a temple to house your sacred love is a co-creative process.
It provides shelter where you can adjust to all life's challenges.

Let your entwined hearts empower you to experience the unity love brings.
You have chosen to take this path together.
May your journey be imbued with the enchanting music of unconditional love.

Work

In our success-driven society, career is central to most of us. Achievements or status in the workplace define our face to the world. Before we realize it, the demands of career take on more and more dominance. Instead of a source of fulfillment of our skills and satisfying income, it becomes the focal point of all our activities, often detracting from marriage and other relationships.

How do we develop a healthy balance between the demands of work and commitments at home? When does work become an addictive relationship, no different than sex or drugs?

For many people, job performance is motivated by dreams they devise for themselves. They fan their passion by making the dreams exciting and enticing, and all the perks that come with professional success. They project fantasies of how they will advance in their career, how much money they will make and what status they will hold in their profession. Fueled by adrenaline and ambition, they climb the ladder of success. They call these dreams "aspirations and career goals." Anything projected into the future, no matter how elevated and purposeful it may seem, is an escape from where they are now.

The self-study of Swadhyaya is necessary to determine this delicate balance for each person. Allowing one's career to consume a disproportionate amount of prana is as destructive as any addiction. The opposite is true when we dread going to work, cannot communicate with the boss or hate the job itself. Apathy, the polar opposite of ambition, sets in. We spend at least one-half of every day engaged in an occupation that can either absorb us or repel us. Both the weight of apathy and drive of ambition dissipate prana, compromising relationships with loved ones as the relationship with our job takes center stage.

Making Light of Hard Work

The conscious approach to work is performing every action in such a total way that nothing feels unfinished or unsatisfied at the end of the day. Every task is thus fulfilled to its capacity due to our focused concentration. This is quite different from the typical outlook on going to work. Imagine adopting this attitude as we head out the door. When we look at our jobs with this totality of focus, we won't come away saying, "I wish that task would have turned out differently" (incompletion), "I handled that situation badly" (regret) or "I never get anything done right or on time" (self-criticism).

Unfinished business and dissatisfaction become part of our unconscious. It manifests as karma. The consequences of karma must always be dealt with at some time in the future. However, if we live each experience fully, nothing is unfinished and nothing is left to be gained. We are complete in our performance without attachment to how it turns out. If we have performed our best, the consequences lie somewhere else. There is no debit on our karma ledger.

It is important to feel energy and passion for work. Otherwise it holds no meaning and is just a preoccupation rather than an occupation. There are two kinds of work-related passion:

1) Goal-oriented—which is created in reaction to an imagined problem or deficiency. It arises from the misperception that we are not enough as we are. The external goal is designed to fill the void. An enormous amount of drive is possible to meet goals, but ultimately there will be disappointment. Even when the goal is met, the feeling of unworthiness remains. There is always more to accomplish to feel satisfied.

2) Love-oriented—which means it doesn't matter what type of work we do as long as we are totally present and en-

gaged every moment. All of us have parts of our job that are not as satisfying as others or those we may even find tedious. Approach those parts with the same energy. Find some pleasure in everything. We derive the greatest fulfillment when all our faculties are drawn into our activities. In the state of absorption, extraordinary satisfaction is a natural by-product.

The Law of Diminishing Return

Dreams become a tranquilizer to ease the pain of a moment that fails to meet our anticipations. When such escape becomes habitual, we are addicted. Some escapes are visible, others not so visible. Some people use sex, drugs or alcohol to escape, others use work or goals. But every addiction is an escape from reality.

Orientation to a goal is disorientation to ourselves, our inner source, the sense of peace and contentment we are longing to find at the end of so much strife. When we focus on a goal, our center moves from something inside to something outside. Running after the goal, we become less and less attuned to the very self for whom the goal was created.

The secret is not to chase after external goals we think will engage use, because the level of absorption we receive from any activity fluctuates according to our state of mind. No external stimulus can consistently provide the same level of enjoyment. Holding on to a peak experience is impossible, yet we continue focusing on achievements. This leaves us unsatisfied because there is always more to accomplish. This is the complete antithesis of the laws of polarity, going up and coming down. Unless we flow with the natural rhythms of polarity, we are caught in the never-ending climb, depleting more and more prana. Even if we possess the Midas touch, the addictive acquisition of more gold is just out of reach. There is no end to it.

What matters is consciousness, rather than the medium through which we are performing.

True satisfaction comes from a deeper level, where doing in itself becomes intrinsically fulfilling. By concentrating on how we do something, we become the creator of our experience, rather than having the experience control us. Then we are not basing satisfaction on the carrot at the end of the stick, but enjoying each bite along the way, savoring the goodness of every moment.

> *Walk the fine line between the drive of a goal-oriented businessperson and the detached concentration of a yogi.*
> *Accept whatever the moment brings.*
> *With practice, it becomes more and more natural.*
>
> *If you maintain focus on how you are, not what you do,*
> *then whatever you do will bring fulfillment.*
> *Fulfillment will flow from your immersion in each moment.*
> *Your life and your work will be carried out with joy and passion for every act you perform.*

Food

Perhaps the least visible but most prevalent dysfunctional relationship is the one we have with food. A major cause of inappropriate consumption is tension, stress and the very metaphorical image of filling the hole in us that we perceive as empty. Unpleasant emotions and bodily tension are a direct drain on prana. To replace lost energy, we turn to the most available and most instant gratification around—the refrigerator, the drive-through or the corner bar.

Eating unwisely may cause a temporary spike in energy as insulin increases or alcohol sooths nerves, but it is always followed by a crash, a lower low than before. Thus begins the cycle of searching for more food or liquor to fill the hole that cannot be satisfied.

This self-defeating cycle is a perfect set-up for unintentional weight gain. Then we have the ideal excuse for not being lovable: *I'm too fat. That's why I'm not in a relationship.* Or why no one will hire us: *I don't fit the profile of how I'm supposed to look on the job. I couldn't do that work anyway with all this extra weight—my back, my legs, my feet hurt!*

Society offers little help in unveiling this unhealthy relationship with what Nature intended as sustenance. Television commercials laud calorie-laden delicacies at restaurants or as close as the microwave. These tantalizing ads are immediately followed by commercials for antacids or the latest celebrity-endorsed weight loss plans. This split personality in a two-minute commercial break is a direct reflection of our emotional state. In this mirror, no other person is required to reflect who you are. The one on the bathroom door is sufficient. We must realize for ourselves that using food to fill our inner emptiness is the sign of spiritual starvation.

Rediscovering Natural Hunger

In this cycle, our over-stimulated appetites have forgotten how to listen to our body's true needs. Instead we only hear our mind's desires for taste to override hidden pain. We have developed eating habits that detract from rather than contribute to our health and well-being. Often we eat when we are not even hungry.

At the root of the problem lies the fact that many people have forgotten the original role of food. Eating is meant to provide nourishment and sustain our life processes so we can explore and develop our higher potentials. We've distorted food's basic function and made it primarily a source of pleasure rather than nurturing our body, which is the same as worshipping the

Divine. That is not to say food was put on the earth for us not to enjoy. Why else would Mother Nature have put the nose just above the mouth, and the two eyes just above that? She knew exactly what she was doing in building a total system of enjoyment of all the fruits of our planet.

As many sages have said, "The body is the temple of the soul." So with every food selection, with every bite, meditate on your temple. How would you treat it? With respect and devotion. Eating quietly and consciousness, how would you nourish your soul? With reverence, gratitude and sacred silence.

There is no one diet that will end spiritual starvation. But self-study, awareness and consciousness will guide each person in how to feed the soul and care for the temple. A simple caveat is to eat half as much and chew twice as long. The body gathers much more prana from food that is chewed consciously, not gulped while engaged in another activity. When you sit down to a meal, just eat. Eat moderately, chew thoroughly and enjoy immensely.

> *Create your diet from your experience of what is best for your health.*
> *Eat in accordance with your prana.*
> *Become conscious of your motivations for eating.*

As you cultivate attitudes toward balanced eating that are supportive of your health, you will receive immediate benefits. You will enjoy the abundance of nourishing foods and gain a richer experience of health and well-being in your life.

Chapter 11

Love as Union

*R*elationship remains life's most mysterious and most enticing phenomenon. Although very few have fathomed its depths, the tools and techniques presented here are a blueprint to exploring what we long for the most: to experience intimacy with others and in the end, reconnect with our true Self.

Following the principles of the Yamas and Niyamas, we will discover that the intimacy we are all looking for is not what we thought it was and it doesn't happen automatically. Real intimacy is bliss. Somewhere deep inside we sense that, but the price of bliss is so high most of us cannot persevere in our search. As we have seen, any sincere attempt to create healthy and intimate relationships is guaranteed to bring up everything we've been running from for an entire lifetime—probably many lifetimes. To be in relationship with others, we must face all that we've been avoiding in ourselves.

Relationships seem so complex because we believe we are dealing with people who are very different from us. Until we recognize that the real complexity comes from having to deal with ourselves we have little chance at creating a meaningful and lasting relationship with another.

The Evolutionary Process

Life's purpose is to lead every soul toward greater consciousness and freedom from limitation. To that end, life has a built-in system that promotes catharsis, the process of encountering and releasing everything we have unconsciously suppressed and is now obscuring our divine potential. Without the self-confrontation that catharsis brings, we would be forever at the mercy of our suppressed pain and repressed fear.

Although suppression is a natural defense mechanism used by all human beings when situations are too intense to handle, our anxieties eventually become tyrants when left unattended. They control our lives in disturbing and restrictive ways. To free ourselves from the tyranny of the unconscious, we must bring its contents out of the darkness and into the light of awareness.

We originally suppressed those aspects of our lives because we found them too frightening or unacceptable to face. And they have remained buried ever since. It is unlikely that we would spontaneously deal with them now. In most cases, we aren't even aware of their existence. This is the critical point where relationships play a transformative role in the Self-discovery process. Relationships have the power to trigger the unconscious, unresolved and non-integrated parts of us.

If their purpose is just to unearth buried pain and create catharsis, surely only the most courageous or masochistic would take the risk of entering relationships. Relationships can reveal our greatest and most wonderful potential, as well as the darkest recesses of our shadow side. Habitually, we try to experience only the parts of us that we like; we also hope to experience only the parts of others that we like. The shadow side is not a place we would willingly wish to investigate. Yet exploration is necessary for evolution.

Most people don't know what they're getting themselves into when they set out to be in relationship. It doesn't matter whether it's a relationship with friends, family members, colleagues or lovers. The basic dynamics are the same. We start out looking for the pleasure of closeness, but sooner or later, life's evolutionary force brings us the opportunity for deeper and more important work. Relationship is the primary medium through which the evolutionary process operates.

Relationship with Source

Ultimately, what each of us is looking for is a connection with our true Self—the Source of all life within us. This Source is the dimension of limitless potential, and its nature is one of love and integration. There is no separation within the Self, only wholeness.

Initially we are attracted to attributes of another because we are actually glimpsing our own unrecognized or undeveloped potential. We like what we see in the mirror of the other. We want to get closer to the other person because we feel as though he or she has something we need.

It's easy to see how we might come to believe that getting what we want, even being who we want to be, depends on getting something from another. Unconsciously, we begin creating relationships with dependency as their foundation. The more out of touch with our Source we are, the more deficient we feel. The more deficient we feel, the more we need friends and lovers we can depend on to give us what we think we're missing. Many of us also look for other people who will depend on us in return. Instead of love or intimacy, what we end up with is codependency. Codependency is accompanied by a misguided sense of exclusivity. We assume that what we find attractive exists within the other, and only within the other.

Love is our true nature; it is who we are beneath all the layers of personality, fear and self-concepts. The experience of love is nothing other than the experience of consciously accessing our Source. How then could it be exclusive? The sun doesn't shine on just a few special people with whom it has chosen to be in relationship. Its nature is to radiate light, give warmth and provide life-sustaining energy. As a result, everyone who comes into its presence can partake of those qualities. The love within our hearts is the same way. Once we remove all the obstructions and know it as our nature, we naturally radiate love to everyone we meet. Therefore, true love can never be exclusive.

We must develop our ability to come from our heart with everyone. Trying to love one or two people while we remain separate from everyone else will never work in the long run.

What is truly attractive is what happens inside us. A friend or loved one can mirror the potential of our Source to us, but he or she does not create what we experience. The challenge is first to recognize the characteristics we glimpse when we are attracted to another as our own potentials, and develop them into qualities we can access whenever we choose. It takes a strong intention to discover the truth of who we really are, an intention that's stronger than our addiction to dependency and exclusivity.

Self-Discovery and Commitment

Love is the divine seed within our hearts. Because it exists within each of us as our highest potential, a life filled with love and intimacy is possible for everyone. No one is excluded. Just as Nature intends for seeds to sprout and produce their fullest bounty, it also intends for us to discover and manifest our own highest potential. Again and again, it gives us opportunities to see ourselves. We do not have to create them; we simply have to learn how to recognize the ones provided. The Self will always lead us toward these opportunities so it can be more fully revealed. This is the evolutionary urge.

To move closer to others we have to begin taking down the walls we've built to protect ourselves—the walls that keep us separate. Once we let down our guard, people invariably reflect to us not only our higher potential, but also everything that stands in the way of realizing it. Those obstructions are the very things we've been trying to avoid: pain, fear, intolerance and insecurity. Not wanting to face those parts of us caused us to build defenses in the first place.

Commitment is necessary if we want to move from superficial relationships to the experience of genuine love and intimacy. To remove the obstructions that block our ability to act from the Source, we must fully experience them as our own and bring them into the light of consciousness. That means we must let go of our protective stances and be honest with ourselves. In the process, we will feel real vulnerability and pain. Without commitment, there is no chance for success.

Relationships that lack commitment as their cornerstone remain in an elementary phase. They get stuck in attempts to avoid pain. The people involved are willing to stay in relationship only as long as it's easy and pleasurable. The relationships are little more than futile attempts to escape from reality. If love is the absolute reality beneath all our defenses and self-images, a relationship that avoids reality takes us in the opposite direction.

Taking the Risk

Choosing love is risky business. We have to stop holding on to comfort as our top priority and acknowledge a higher purpose for our lives.

Most of us confuse freedom with escape. We want to be free—liberated from suffering, separation and limitation—but we don't realize that the real obstacles exist inside us. So, in the name of freedom, we do everything we can to escape discomfort, responsibility and commitment—the life experiences that could help us most.

Freedom is not a matter of escaping from reality. We do not eliminate our fears and weaknesses by refusing to experience them. Just the opposite. Through avoidance, we reinforce them. They continue to live in the darkness of the unconscious and influence everything we do. They even convince us to create our lives in such a way that we don't ever have to encounter them directly. But when we manipulate our world just so we can avoid facing the parts of us we don't like, we do ourselves a great disservice. We allow fear to keep us imprisoned within the limits of our defensive mental habits, eliminating the possibility for Self-discovery.

Keys to Relationship

Adhering to the Yamas and Niyamas, not daily, but in every moment, is the secret to finding the love we seek and the relationships we long for. In this practice, there can be no failure as we continue to learn from our experiences and regard all relationships as opportunities to further our personal growth and spiritual development. Successful observance is enhanced by remembering these five keys:

The first key is commitment. A steadfast resolve to love, truth, consciousness and integration sharpens our awareness of when we are out of alignment with our core values. It is easier to recognize when we are acting unconsciously, so we can return to being conscious.

The second key is practice. Without regular practice, it's very easy to be thrown by the conflicts and challenges in our lives. We can't afford to wait for major crises in our relationships to start being conscious. Daily, willful practice builds the psychological and spiritual muscles we need.

The third key is containment. Containment means holding the energy of any experience inside us, rather than immediately reacting in some habitual way to discharge it. If we can contain and experience the energy, we can create a gap between a stimulus and our pre-programmed, defensive response. We can give ourselves the chance to see more clearly and act from a place of choice rather than conditioning.

The fourth key is compassion. We cannot use relationship for Self-discovery unless we have compassion for ourselves and others. If we enter into relationship, we will definitely see our faults, as well as the faults of our loved ones. No one is perfect. We must always remember that we are evolving souls and suspend our inclination to judge or blame.

The fifth key is surrender. The only way to be free from our internal blocks is to stop being "right." That means we have to be willing to let go of identification with the ego's version of reality. The death of the ego only appears painful but it is just anticipated fear. When the ego actually surrenders, it is the most ecstatic liberation an individual can ever experience. Otherwise, we will be locked into all our habitual patterns, and instead of growing, find ourselves perpetually stuck in the past.

The Fieldwork for Spirituality

We all have to relate to other people: husbands, wives, parents, children, neighbors, business associates and friends. Where life is trying to provide the next evolutionary step, there will often be catharsis, and each person involved will feel the disturbance. At that time we have a choice. We can deny our own role in the conflict, or we can choose to enter the opportunity consciously.

Relationship with others is the fieldwork for spirituality. It is the most important *sadhana* we can do. Spiritual practice does not belong in some separate corner of our lives; it must touch every part of our existence.

All the different relationships we find ourselves in are not really separate after all. Ultimately there is only one relationship for any of us, and that's the relationship we have with the Self. We may play many different roles in our lives, but each becomes *dharma*—the highest and truest path—when we use it to bring about deeper integration with our Source.

This brings us to the final Niyama—*Ishvara Pranidhana*. Concentrating all our efforts toward personal growth, dedicating our lives to the service of others and surrendering it all to the Divine is truly our return to the Soul. When every act is performed with devotion to our Higher Self, the relationship is consummated.

Om Namo Bhagavate Vasudevaya

Thy will be done, Lord, not mine.

Appendices

Yamas and Niyamas: Guidelines for Day-to-Day Living

The Yamas and Niyamas are the first two limbs of the eightfold Ashtanga Yoga, as set down by Yogi Patanjali (circa 2nd Century BC). Known today as the *Yoga Sutras*, his is the first written record of yogic practices. Prior to Patanjali, these sacred esoteric teachings were passed down by word of mouth, from teacher (rishi) to deserving student (shishya). Patanjali has left us a great yet mysterious gift. He outlines the following principles in Sutra II:30.

Yamas—Observances
Ahimsa—*non-violence*
Satya—*non-lying*
Asteya—*non-stealing*
Brahmacharya—*moderation*
Aparigraha—*non-attachment*

Niyamas—Disciplines
Saucha—*purity*
Santosha—*contentment*
Tapas—*spiritual heat*
Swadhyaya—*self-study*
Ishvara Pranidhana—
surrender to the Divine

The Yamas and Niyamas are the foundation of both Hatha and Raja Yoga, and the basis for spiritual life. These ancient truths are as applicable today as they were in the days of Patanjali. The science of yoga is applied to our lives by examining unconscious habits, beliefs and behaviors... and their consequences.

Too often, these universal principles have been reduced to the man-made concepts of virtues and vices, but they are not to be interpreted as conventional ethics or religious codes of morality. Integrating the values of the Yamas and Niyamas is not aimed at making us socially acceptable law-abiding citizens, but at facilitating an internal shift for inner transformation.

Morality and ethics can be adapted superficially while values remain dualistic. When idealistic concepts and religious behavior are merely adapted, they become a fanatic belief system, not integration.

If the spiritual principles are practiced as do's and don'ts, an inherent danger of guilt and self-rejection accompanies such unrealistic goals. Self-judgment always arises if we fail in one of the disciplines, which is likely to be a daily occurrence. Self-righteous attitudes turn into masks that obscure rather than reveal the Self. Behavior modifications that are adapted rather than sourced are inauthentic. Even the Yamas and Niyamas, if not practiced with mindful meditative awareness, can themselves become the cause of conflict.

Their purpose is to eliminate disturbances that come from within and without. They are not about reformation of the self-image, but about transformation and Self-discovery. They purify the body, mind and heart, while developing witness consciousness. Practiced through the medium of witness consciousness rather than from the judgmental seat of right or wrong, the meditative approach embraces all opposites. We must be willing to drop the barriers of the self-image and living in reaction if we are to awaken to reality. Once we practice the Yamas and Niyamas in their true spirit, we naturally perform the posture of consciousness in all our actions.

The Yamas—Observances

Ahimsa

Ahimsa's top position signifies its primary importance. It is the very seed of the disciplines that follow. Ahimsa is more than the absence of violence. It is seeing through the eyes of love, acceptance of self and others, and exercising kindness, tolerance and consideration. It is called non-violence because we have no way of understanding what true love is, but we do know what it is not. Because we do not know what real love is, we automatically practice what we imagine it is. As a result, we miss the spirit of love and become the victims of our misguided concepts. This is why *rishis*, in their wisdom, defined love as ahimsa.

Violence can be present in either gross or subtle forms. When we are physically violent or express aggressive words or feelings, it is in its gross form. When we think angry thoughts, it is a subtle form of violence. Ahimsa must be applied to all thoughts, words and actions.

In yoga, we practice ahimsa both on and off the yoga mat. We are attentive to our attitudes, beliefs and speech and their subsequent impact. During the practice of postures, we do not become forceful with our body. We remain internally aware, dismissing self-critical mental comments. We accept ourselves as we are in the moment, without the need to deny our perceived shortcomings.

Ahimsa is the state that exists when all violence in the heart and mind have subsided. It is not something we have to acquire; it is always present and only needs to be uncovered. When one practices ahimsa, one refrains from causing distress—in thought, word or deed—to any living creature, including oneself.

Swami Kripalvanandji

Satya

Satya is truth that extends beyond not telling lies. If we live in truth, all parts of our being harmoniously function with one voice. When what we feel is different from what we think and when we do something different from what we feel or think, we are out of integrity with ourselves and the world.

Unconsciously motivated thoughts, speech and actions emerge from unresolved issues. Buried unconscious issues represent personal self-concepts that are in conflict with impersonal reality. Every conflict with reality is the same as lying to what is. When we identify with the self-image, we are not being truthful to the all-pervading universal Self. In truth, we are integrated, whole and undivided.

We need not worry about practicing truth in speech, but merely need to delete a little untruth from the mass of untruth we usually speak.

Swami Kripalvanandji

We cannot be truthful and at the same time be identified with who we are not. This is our ability to see the truth—to see reality. Connecting with the true Self transcends the preprogrammed filters of the self-image.

Asteya

Asteya is not taking anything that does not belong to us, a paradigm that far exceeds tangible property. The underlying premise of coveting is the belief that we are insufficient. Asteya is an affirmation that we need nothing outside of ourselves to feel complete.

When we obtain what we desire by honest means, our mind remains at peace and free of fear. Non-stealing is not desiring anyone's wealth by thought, word or deed, as well as not taking anyone's possessions, no matter how small, without their permission.
Swami Kripalvanandji

All deficiencies are perceived deficiencies. Believing that solutions come from external sources, we desire what others have to make us feel whole. This is where subtle stealing, jealousy and competition are born. Once established in the knowledge that the source of both problems and solutions lie within, we realize that our inherent potential cannot be stolen. We are enough as we are.

Beginning our spiritual journey with this core realization, greed for what we perceive is missing gradually diminishes. Simultaneously our connection with the infinite source of creativity, intuition, strength and wisdom is reinforced. Access to the kingdom of heaven within is ours for the taking.

Brahmacharya

The literal translation of brahmacharya is to move toward Brahman, returning to the Source. By exercising brahmacharya, we progressively drop habits and activities that keep us apart from our true nature. Any form of excessive sensual indulgences that deplete our vitality, our life force or our shakti, prevent us from accessing the Source.

Often brahmacharya is translated as celibacy. This approach is for the renunciate. For the worldly person, bramacharya is moderation and conservation of sexual and sensual energy with the intention to be in tune with Truth, Reality and God—the cultivation of the creative life force within. It is not a dogmatic ideal that leads to guilt and self-rejection. It is a choice to consciously manage all out-flowing energies. The problem with sex is not biological but its accompanying emotions, addictions and dependencies. Our psychological appetites drag us into excessive indulgence in sensual pleasures.

> *Brahamcharya means not indulging in sensuality, thoughts or emotions that drain your vital life force, the powerful vehicle for Self-realization.*

As a Yama, brahmacharya helps us cultivate thoughts and actions to increase our understanding of the conservation of shakti and its relationship to the Higher Self. This takes vigilance. Again and again, we must let go of all unconscious disturbances that could take us off center. With continued practice, we progressively move toward the higher centers of consciousness.

Aparigraha

Aparigraha is letting go of fear-based attachments. Fear invariably drives us toward objects of attachments as protection. Attachments represent unconscious fears. Addictions to possessions represent greed. All hoarding and clinging are fear- and security-based. Fear can provide us with motivation for developing resources, but fear that becomes accumulating can be released only when we become Sourceful instead of resourceful.

As we reflect on our lives in relation to aparigraha, we recognize our tendency to cling to objects, people, places, thoughts, beliefs, feelings and situations. If we look deeply at our desire to cling or hoard, we can see the origins of these tendencies. We may feel strongly attracted to a person. Behind the attraction is fear of losing that person, which leads to obsessive attachment. By observing ourselves, we begin to feel the burden attachments create and are ultimately able to consciously release them.

When we practice aparigraha, our mechanical, mental and emotional habits of attractions and repulsions are revealed in the light of consciousness, providing us with the opportunity to let them go.

The Niyamas—Disciplines

Saucha

In Sanskrit, saucha represents two types of purity: external (physical) and internal (mental). Applications of saucha on the physical level include cleanliness, orderliness of surroundings, proper diet, pranayama, postures, right livelihood and adherence to the Yamas and Niyamas. Physical purification sanctifies our bodies, hearts and minds. Internal purification is impacted by physical sanctity, but is dependent on meditative awareness and self-observation.

Saucha also means sacredness or holiness. Keeping this in mind, the disciplines of purification become an act of devotion, a way of loving, respecting and taking care of ourselves with heartfelt reverence.

Saucha is practiced from a place of insightful awareness. Embodied purity reflects itself in the way we experience ourselves and in our interactions. It spiritualizes and transforms every expression and expands our view of life with compassion, love and selfless service.

The internal aspect of saucha focuses on awareness of toxic emotions and attitudes, especially the habit of indulging in negative thinking such as self-criticism and emotion. When we bring the destructive impact of self-defeating thoughts to our awareness, we have the power to rid them from our consciousness.

The practice of purity involves more than having a healthy body through proper diet, cleanliness and exercise. It also means cultivating a wholesome mind through positive thinking, good company, prayer and meditation. Virtuous conduct is the chief characteristic of mental purity since one can act virtuously only when the mind is pure.

Swami Kripalvanandji

Our intention is to heal our body, clear our mind and purify our heart, bringing them into alignment with our highest potential, not by suppression, but by acceptance. As we cease to fuel thoughts by identifying with them, fighting with them or denying them, they die of starvation. We are left with the awareness of our inherent innocence, purity and wholeness.

Santosha

Santosha is contentment, the ability to tolerate and digest the opposing experiences of duality with the equanimity of the ocean. Even though all rivers flood into it, the ocean remains unperturbed. Similarly, the yogi lives in the world, yet remains content at every moment, despite the ebbs and flows of life.

Santosha is unconditional. Being free from addictions and fears creates an objective state without personal preferences for or against what is present. Established in the changeless state of awareness, we embrace all opposing experiences.

The movement of duality is circular. What goes up comes down. What goes down is destined to go up again. Santosha is the hub of the wheel, remaining a steady center around which all the opposing experiences move through conflicting dualities. That is why the world is described as Samsara Chakra, the wheel of life. Santosha is the direct result of remaining a changeless witness to all the opposing experiences of the phenomenal world. Changeless is the non-doing state of being.

When we are aligned with santosha, we are not anxious to get somewhere. There is no stress, so we are fully present with being in the present. Santosha creates an entry to the dimension of grace that comes not from doing something to get somewhere but from being in the undivided, timeless state of the now. Being in the now does not require any doing or desire for change.

> *When we are not seeking excitement, life becomes exciting in a very deep way. It is joy without excitement. Then, when excitement comes, it is not like a rushing river, but like deep still water—where there is hardly any movement on the surface.*

Santosha is an adventurous journey that demands everything we have to arrive here and now. It does not demand security; it demands fearlessness. When our attention is divided between now and the future, our ability to function effectively is greatly reduced. Being present is productive, not passive. When we are totally present, our capacity to enjoy what we are doing happens naturally all along the way rather than at the end of the journey.

Only in the absence of anxiety can we live in the present with love, faith and trust. This creates compassion rather than frustration with the world and its events. Compassion is the most powerful way to serve humanity. When motivated by fear, even the search for peace turns into war.

Tapas

Tapas is spiritual heat generated by the process of releasing our self-image, so that the true Self may begin to surface. This is practiced through continual evenness (abhyasa) and non-attachment (vairagya) when we find ourselves being most reactive.

In the *Bhagavad Gita*, Lord Krishna speaks of the three types of spiritual heat: tapas of the body, of speech and of the mind: "Just as fire purifies gold, restraint or discipline purifies the body, mind and heart of the seeker."

Whenever we sense threats, our instincts of self-preservation react with the fight or flight reflex. Even if it is a perceived threat, instinct reacts as if it were real. Survival reactions, whether for the protection of the physical self or the self-image, are both unconscious and instinctive.

The ego prevents tapas by finding different ways to release pain as a temporary escape mechanism rather than resolve the cause of the pain. The ego takes one or more of the following measures to avoid addressing the real source of the problem:

- *fights to save our self-image*
- *resists and runs away*
- *blames someone else for causing our suffering*
- *shames us with guilt*

When we are reactive, we must relax, breathe and let go to create a space between the point of impact that ignites the reaction and the reactive action. It is in this window of transformation that we experience tapas. The only way to create this space is to remain witness to our first reaction.

Every time we choose not to react to our reactions or act out our reactions, we starve the self-image. If we fight it, we feed it. If we run from it, we feed it. Only when we remain the observer can we deny it food to perpetuate itself. The dying process of the self-image ignites the spiritual heat. Tapas is the alchemy where the unconscious is turned into consciousness.

> *To purify the mind, the average seeker should begin by attempting to accomplish tapas of the body. Tapas of speech and tapas of the mind will automatically follow.*
>
> Swami Kripalvanandji

Swadhyaya

Swadhyaya is the study of the self, leading to the deeper connection with our true Self. Transformation and healing is founded on introspection and self-observation, where all unconscious beliefs are clearly exposed in the light of consciousness.

> *I will give you one secret. Whatever you seek in life, you will find through this practice. Just learn self-observation. By this practice, you will be able to master your mind, your intellect and your ego. It is the surest and easiest way to progress.*
>
> Swami Kripalvanandji

While performing everyday activities, we must allow just a part of the mind to observe ourselves objectively. At first, we will only see our faults and inferior qualities, which is why we must always observe ourselves without judgment. By and by, we begin to notice good qualities, as well. By focusing less on lower characteristics, the higher ones occur more naturally and with more frequency. Still we must not hide from our faults. New ones will continue to reveal themselves if we allow them. When we are willing to see all our dark qualities without shame, our natural goodness comes forth without effort.

Diligent study and contemplation of yogic scriptures, as well as the teachings of the realized masters, can also enhance our self-knowledge. They support each other and open our minds and hearts to the limitless potential we have at all times—if we only just remember.

Ishvara Pranidhana

Ishvara Pranidhana is dedication of all the consequences of our actions to the Divine. Ego-driven actions are goal-oriented and performed for an expected outcome. Letting go of the end results requires complete faith in the absence of fear or need to control. The *Bhagavad Gita* says, "The Lord abides in the heart region of all beings. To surrender means to dedicate one's every thought, word and deed to the Lord."

Mindful meditative focus helps us disengage from personal biases. Each time we let go of fears and attachments, we automatically surrender to the Lord within. With an attitude of surrendering the results, actions lose their capacity to produce emotional reactions and mental agitations.

Being disengaged from addiction to success frees the mind from agitation and the heart from emotional reaction. Energy and attention released from unconscious preoccupation becomes available for whatever we are doing in the present moment.

When our mind is peaceful and our body is relaxed,
we remain free from preoccupation with anxiety and fear.

When we are totally engaged in whatever we are doing,
the experience is deeply fulfilling and satisfying.

When we are disengaged from attachment to our dreams,
we are not driven by impatience, self-doubt or stress.

When we are present,
fulfillment happens all along the way.

The consequences of our actions are essentially the function of the law of karma. Giving up attachment to the end result, the mind becomes tranquil yet alert; its faculties are activated to function optimally and creatively. Thereby, we disrupt the chain of new karma that comes with attractions and repulsions. By surrendering personal addictions and fears, we are also free from the consequences of success and failure.

Ishvara Pranidhana empowers us to live in complete freedom, unaffected by the unknown. Love, trust and faith must first arise in one's own heart before it can possibly be surrendered to the Lord.

> *Only a lit lamp can light an unlit lamp. If we perform one hundred actions for ourselves everyday, can't we perform one or two actions for our beloved Lord who is our true relative and well-wisher? After all, actions dedicated to ourselves are useless actions and bring only pain; but actions dedicated to the Lord are genuine actions and bring true happiness.*
>
> Swami Kripalvanandji

Meditation on Healing Relationships

Sit quietly in a space where you will not be disturbed for the next 30 minutes. Assume a comfortable position to enable yourself to enter a receptive mode where you realize the in-depth secrets of relationships. This awareness allows you to view your relationship as healing and awakening at the same time.

Take a few deep breaths with this intention.
Focus on the inhalation as it reaches the depths of your abdomen, pause.
Release it slowly through your nostrils.
Let the breathing take you into deeper relaxation.
Sense the calmness in your mind and create an opening for healing.
Let relaxation take you beyond any issues in your relationship.
Drop any judgments, resentments or expectations.

You can alter the programming that has been reinforced in the past.
As you move closer toward your Source, you enter a realm where profound changes happen spontaneously.
Know that superficial changes are not the answer.
Seek not the reformation of your relationship, but the transformation of your being.

Now breathe normally.
Being firmly established in the consciousness from where you can perceive the relationship independent of your past or dreams of how it should be,
Real transformation is possible.
New possibilities exist beyond your mind.
They have the potential to shower you with joy and freedom of intimacy through relationship.

In order to heal, the first step is to let go of all the conclusions you have made in your mind about your interactions with the other.

Be willing to see your relationship from a state of consciousness where there is no blame and no shame.
Realize that only through love can you experience the intimacy you desire.

The moment you demand love, it disappears.
Be willing to drop all the subtle demands you have of the other.

In front of your mind's eye, invoke the presence of your beloved.
Visualize your lover in the center of your inner eye standing before you.
Notice that no judgments arise in your mind...all defensiveness, guilt and resentment dissolve as you gaze with loving eyes at the form of your beloved.

If unwanted feelings disrupt your gaze, visualize those feelings as balloons.
Puncture each one and deflate them one by one.
Feel the power of any negativity dissipating into the air.

Visualize a glow of light surrounding your loved one.
Send a beam of light emerging directly from your heart to the heart of the other.
See it. Feel it. Allow its warmth to flow through your being.
A golden glow surrounds you both, with a cord of light uniting your hearts.
No thoughts or feelings can disrupt the beam.
You are deeply connected from heart to heart.

Tell your partner with all honesty and objectivity all that you want to drop;
All that is standing in the way of harmony between you.
Say all that you have been avoiding from fear of repercussion.
Admit your fear of being misunderstood.
Express the ways in which you may have hurt the other.
In doing so, feel your heart open even more.

Let your conversation emerge from an open heart that is free from expectations.
Regaining clarity in your relationship, feel the beam of light progressively
grow stronger.

Remind yourself of all the ways your partner has attempted to love you.
Understand that behind any criticism, the intention to love you remained.
Consciously recognize that intention and let go of any anger, insult or fear.
Think of all the times you have felt love from the other. . .go through every event as
if it were happening now.
Experience the intimacy and be grateful.

Recognize and affirm that you are not separate from your beloved.
As you give love to another, you give love to yourself.
There is no difference between you.
Use this relationship to see yourself rather than hide behind it.

At this moment, drop all dreams of how love should be.
All that you give comes back in manifold form.
Make a commitment that through this relationship, you intend to grow in love.

In a conscious relationship, love makes a complete circle.
It is not just loving the other or only yourself.
You are responsible for what you create.
Do not hold the other responsible for what happens to you.
In so doing, you return to the Source of love that is within you.

Shanti Shanti OM

*The complete recording with Yogi Desai's voice in meditation is
available at www.amritkala.com.*

Glossary

Editor's Note: Not all of the terms listed are in this book, but are prevalent in the works and teachings of Yogi Desai. His definitions are provided here to broaden understanding of his interpretation of esoteric yogic principles.

Abhyasa—*having an attitude of persistent effort to attain and maintain a state of stable tranquility; practiced along with Vairagya, non-attachment.*

Acceptance–*ceasing resistance; absence of reaction to what is present in reality.*

Ahimsa—*non-violence; the 1st Yama; see commentary.*

Ama—*toxins held in the body.*

Amrita—*from Hindu mythology, the nectar of life. Amrita is the drink of immortality, the ultimate stage yogis aspire to. Amrita metaphorically resides in the pineal gland; the divine elixir that heals all human suffering caused by separative consciousness.*

Aparigraha—*non-attachment; the 5th Yama; see commentary.*

Asanas—*hatha yoga postures.*

Ashtanga—*the eight-limbed yoga system as explained in the Yoga Sutras codified by Patanjali circa the 2nd century BC.*

Asteya—*non-stealing; the 3rd Yama; see commentary.*

Atman—*Soul, Higher Self, eternal Source.*

Avatar—*an incarnation of God.*

Avidya—*illusion; ignorance of reality.*

Awareness–*represents the meditative perception of reality without personal bias.*

Bhagavad Gita—*The Song of the Lord; epic tale depicting Krishna's discourse to his beloved disciple, Arjuna, as he prepares to go into battle against his own relatives.*

Brahmacharya—*moderation of senses; the 3rd Yama; see commentary.*

Bhakti Yoga—*the yoga of love, devotion and selfless service.*

Chakras—*the seven centers (wheels) of energy/consciousness located in the subtle body, where we receive, transmit and process life energies (see prana). The chakras are astral centers, corresponding to the nerve plexuses in the spine. Each chakra has specific characteristics corresponding to a particular state of consciousness.*

Choiceless awareness *(see witness consciousness).*

Darshan—*an audience with a spiritual master or a saint.*

Dharma—*spiritual truth, natural law; the way of truth.*

Dharna—*concentration; one of the eight limbs of Ashtanga Yoga; part of the mental discipline of Raja Yoga.*

Dhyana—*meditation; one of the eight limbs of Ashtanga Yoga. It is the window for the entrance to the spiritual dimension of the discipline of Ashtanga Yoga.*

Direct experience—*experiencing directly without the interference or distortion from pre-programmed personal biases; experience beyond the rational mind with the beginner's mind, which is received at a cellular level.*

Duality—*when natural polarity is altered by personal preferences for or against what is present, it becomes duality. Through this personal preference, the complementary polarity in nature becomes conflicting duality for those who attempt to separate one pole from the other, which is experienced as internal conflict (see polarity).*

Ecstasy—*derived from the Greek, "to stand outside of oneself." In yoga, it is the ultimate orgasmic experience of the union of Shiva* and *Shakti, known as Samadhi. It is union with the Self that has been completely liberated from the limitations of the self-image.*

Ego—*the self-image, which comes to us through the mind and our pre-programmed self-concepts and belief systems.*

Experiential *(see direct experience)*

Hatha Yoga–*represents a physical component of the mental and spiritual discipline of Raja Yoga. Together, they form Patanjali's classical system of eight-limbed Ashtanga Yoga.*

Integration—*the process of bringing together the physical, mental, emotional and spiritual bodies to function in complete balance and harmony. Integration (union) is the ultimate purpose of the practice of yoga.*

Ishvara Pranidhana—*surrender to the Divine; the 5th Niyama; see commentary.*

Japa—*recitation of mantra in conjunction with counting mala (prayer) beads.*

Karma—*the law of cause and effect: every action has an opposite and equal reaction. "As you sow, so shall you reap." Karma is unresolved, incomplete experiences of the past, returning again and again in the present, giving us new opportunities to encounter it consciously and resolve it. The action we perform is called karma and the reaction to the action is the result of karma.*

Kriyas—*spontaneous physical manifestations directly activated by awakened Kundalini in the form of Hatha Yoga postures, pranayamas, locks, mudras and cleansing kriyas, leading toward the highest state of Samadhi.*

Kundalini—*the primordial cosmic energy that lies coiled at the base of the spine. When awakened, Kundalini begins to move upward, penetrating the chakras and initiating various yogic kriyas,* *which bring about total purification, rejuvenation and transformation of the entire being, leading to the ultimate state of Samadhi, the state of immortality.*

Mantra—*powerful sound vibrations which, when chanted continuously, have a calming and purifying effect on the nervous system, mind and heart; sacred sounds of power which release potent spiritual energies within the chanter; a sacred incantation.*

Maya—*the illusion of the material plane.*

Meditation—*objective impersonal observation of whatever becomes the object of our awareness; the development of non-judgmental witness which allows us to embrace opposites unconditionally and takes us from the field of duality to the sacred state of unity and oneness.*

Meditative Awareness *(see witness consciousness)*

Moksha—*enlightenment, liberation; absolute freedom; awakening of the Self.*

Mudras—*various hand gestures and physical positions prompted spontaneously by awakened Kundalini that create internal movement of energies to break through blockages in the physical, mental and emotional bodies.*

Mukti—*another term for liberation.*

Nadi Shuddhi—*through consistent practice of asanas, pranayama, diet and balanced living, the body becomes relaxed, nerve channels are refined, blood is purified, the mind is clear and calm and the heart is open and receptive to subtler vibrations. Its purity radiates through sparkling eyes, clear radiant countenance and luminosity of the skin.*

Nivritti Marg—*yogic path of renunciation.*

Nirvikalpa Samadhi—*complete absorption; the thought-less formless state of being.*

Om—*the primordial sound of the Universe, which represents unity; the essence of all mantras.*

Patanjali—*often called the Father of Yoga; first to formally record yogic practices as the eight limbs of yoga, circa 200 BC; his exposition is called the Yoga Sutras.*

Polarity—*in nature, polarity is complementary and operates in harmony as a unit (one pole cannot exist without the other); it exists in the form of attraction and repulsion, birth and death, expansion and contraction (see duality).*

Prana—*the primal intelligent energy that regulates the macrocosm of the entire universe as well as the universe in microcosm—the human body; represents the soul as well as the vital breath.*

Prana pranotthana—*postures performed automatically when prana has been awakened in the body of a yogi; this is the entrance into Kundalini yoga.*

Pranav—*chanting of OM with a closed mouth.*

Pranayama—*breathing techniques that regulate, control and restrain the breath; one of the disciplines of yoga that extends the power of prana.*

Prasad—*the sweet food given in love by the master to his disciple.*

Pratyahara—*retrieving outgoing attention, one of the eight limbs of Ashtanga Yoga.*

Pravritti Marg—*yogic path of one who is married.*

Puja—*rituals of worship.*

Rajas—*highly stimulated energy.*

Raja Yoga—*the mental discipline of yoga.*

Rishi—*ancient yogi, seer who has a direct experience or perception of God.*

Sadhana—*one's spiritual practices; dharmic path.*

Saha—*the mundane world; the physical plane.*

Samadhi—*the 8th limb of Ashtanga Yoga; the final experience of the ultimate union of the individual soul with the cosmic soul.*

Samsara Chakra—*the wheel of life.*

Sankalpa—*intention; one's resolve.*

Santosha—*contentment; the 2nd Niyama; see commentary.*

Satsang—*in the company of truth (literal); a devotional gathering.*

Sattva—*balance in energy.*

Satya—*non-lying; the 2nd Yama; see commentary.*

Saucha—*purity, the 1st Niyama; see commentary.*

Savikalpa Samadhi—*meditation experience of bliss but with awareness of the object of experience; the beginning stage of Samadhi.*

Self—*denotes both the Supreme soul as well as the individual soul; according to ancient Vedic scriptures, both are identical.*

Self-Discovery—*the process of disassociation from identification with our self-image; uncovering the layers of the self-image that simultaneously reveals the Self.*

Sensation (bodily)—*ability to feel what is present without the pre-programmed preference for or against the experience; it is a felt-sense experience.*

Separative Ego—*The self-image, which is born of our self-concepts. When we identify with our self-image as our true self, we are separated from ourselves, from others and from our Higher Self.*

Seva—*selfless service; fosters an attitude of selflessness and spiritual awareness.*

Shakti—*the female force or energy. It is the divine cosmic energy,* *which projects, maintains and dissolves the universe; portrayed as the universal mother.*

Shanti—*peace.*

Shiva—*supreme consciousness; also a name for the all-pervasive supreme reality; one of the Hindu trinity, representing the process of transformation.*

Shiva Netra—*see Third Eye*

Shushumna—*subtle nerve channel within the spinal column, extending from the base of the spine to the brain through which awakened Kundalini rises; it is the pathway to the ultimate experience of yoga.*

Surrender—*letting go of the ego (self); willingness to be open and to wholeheartedly embrace all experiences without judgment; letting go of all that holds us back from being one with our divine Self.*

Sutra—*thread, a line of thought.*

Swadhyaya—*self-study, the 4th Niyama; see commentary.*

Swasthya—*ultimate health; being established in the inborn self-generative, self-healing power of our physical, mental and emotional bodies.*

Tamas—*sluggish body energy*

Tapas—*the burning of unconscious activities; the 3rd Niyama; see commentary.*

Third Eye—*the sacred spot between the eyebrows where integration occurs; its location is the sixth chakra.*

Upanishads—*summaries of the teachings in the Vedas; the Amrit Yoga opening prayer is from this scripture.*

Vairagya—*non-attachment; a dual practice with Abhyasa.*

Vedas—*the four ancient scriptures upon which Hinduism is based; also knowledge, wisdom.*

Witness Consciousness—*non-participative choiceless awareness or meditative awareness; the non-judgmental, impersonal observer.*

Yamas and Niyamas–*abstentions and guidelines that prevent distractions and disturbances that come from within and from without.*

Yoga—*union of the individual soul with the cosmic soul; the ecstatic experience of the union of Shiva and Shakti; the state of oneness with the Higher Self.*

Yoga Nidra—*a conscious connection with your subconscious where you enter the alpha state; where the mystical powers of the third eye are released, actualizing the healing power of affirmations, visualizations and prayers.*

.

About the Author

Yogi Amrit Desai

Yogi Amrit Desai is widely recognized as one of the leading authorities on yoga and holistic living. As a teacher, his special gift is his unique ability to present profound essential yogic wisdom as a practical method anyone can adopt. His very presence radiates the inner warmth, divine joy and spiritual energy that are the outward expressions of awakened consciousness.

Yogi Desai's spiritual odyssey began at 16 in Gujarat, a rural western state in India. At that time, his Guru, Sri Swami Kripalvanandji recognized that the young Amrit possessed special gifts as a spiritual teacher. As a result of his Kundalini awakening in 1970, Yogi Desai directly realized the unity within all life and the divine essence within each of us. This experience became the basis of the work he called Kripalu Yoga, Meditation in Motion, in honor of his Guru. In this work, he refined methodologies that shattered the current notions of yoga as a physical discipline and opened the way for participants to embark on a path of self-discovery and enlightenment through the practice of yoga and meditation.

Immigrating to the U.S. in 1960 to study at the Philadelphia College of Art, he soon realized his true calling lay in the teachings of yoga. He founded a Yoga Ashram in Sumneytown, PA, that later grew into the Kripalu Center for Yoga and Health, the largest center of its kind in North America. For the next 20 years he continued developing this yoga system. Today, his methodology is taught and practiced by thousands of people around the world.

At age 82, Yogi Desai remains an invigorating force, continually refining his technique and teachings to meet the needs of our ever-evolving world. He is often in residence at the Amrit Yoga Institute in Salt Springs, Florida. The institute is a sanctuary for seekers, offering year-round, seminars, retreats and intensive courses in meditation, yoga nidra and yoga teacher training.

Yogi Desai is neither a philosopher nor a psychologist. He represents a mystic, Tantric tradition, imparting energetic experience through direct transmission. He is a Master whose presence creates a palpable energetic field where synergy transports one to a state of consciousness, stillness, peace and tranquility.

Amrit Yoga Institute • www.amrityoga.org • 352-685-3001